Housing Finance

a basic guide

Henry Aughton
with
Peter Malpass

Third revised edition

A Shelter Publication

Third revised edition
Published in 1990 by Shelter, 88 Old Street, London EC1V 9HU

British Library Cataloguing in Publication Data

Aughton, Henry
Housing finance : a basic guide. -3rd. ed.
1. England. Housing. Finance
I. Title II. Malpass, Peter
338.4336350942

ISBN 1-870767-00-4

Cover design by Sue Tong
Cartoons by Brick
Designed by Rahila Gupta, Shelter
Layout by PDP, London WC1X 9NT, Tel:071-837 3782
Printed by Russell Press Ltd., Nottingham NG7 4ET

Trade Distribution by Turnaround, 27 Horsell Road, London N5
1XL. Tel: 071-609 7568

cknowledgements

Roger Matthews, a former head of Shelter's Research and Information section, was a mine of financial, legal and statistical information, and gave inestimable help with the earlier editions. I want to take this opportunity of saying how much I value it.

Peter Malpass, principal lecturer in housing policy at Bristol Polytechnic provided unlimited expertise in all aspects of housing policy and finance. His guidance through the jungle of new legislation and directions and, even more, his insight into underlying policies and intentions, has been invaluable.

Carol Grant, the editor of ROOF, gave unstinting support. I cannot thank her enough for the gratifying results of her editing and the brisk and competent way she dealt with my many sins of omission and commission.

Finally, there is Angela Findlay who has discharged the daunting task of preparing the manuscript for the printers with admirable patience, speed and efficiency.

Henry Aughton
1990

Note about the author

Henry Aughton has a background in both housing and finance. He was Hemel Hempstead's Borough Treasurer for 14 years and subsequently Dacorum District Council's first Chief Executive. Altogether, he has had 47 years experience in local government. He was housing adviser to the Association of Municipal Corporations and specialist adviser in 1977 and 1978 to the House of Commons Environment Sub-Committee. He has also served on housing working parties of the Chartered Institute of Public Finance and Accountancy and was, for many years, Deputy Chair of Shelter and Chair of its finance committee. He is currently Honorary Treasurer of the National Housing and Town Planning Council.

List of Tables

ontents

Chapter 8

Reform — what next?

Index

oreword

It ain't what people don't know that causes trouble.
It's what they know that ain't so.
Mark Twain (1835 — 1910)

This basic guide was first published in 1981, and updated in 1986.

Since then, fundamental changes have been made by the Housing Act 1988, and the Local Government and Housing Act 1989. Together they will far exceed anything affecting housing since that first major piece of legislation, the Housing Act 1919.

The purpose of this guide, like its earlier versions, is to describe how housing finance works in England and Wales, and what the future will hold.

Housing finance is regarded by most people as impossibly complicated, and most published work on the subject, although valuable to housing professionals, may reinforce that perception. Yet the ordinary individual already has, unconsciously, a useful store of background knowledge. Provided that jargon and technicalities are avoided, they can make their own assessment of issues, see how present systems work, and form judgements as to the value of proposed changes.

This guide aims to help in that process. It is not intended primarily for those seeking professional qualifications, though they may find it a useful beginning. It is aimed at councillors, members of housing association management committees, those working in housing or finance departments, housing advice workers, perhaps even MPs — in fact anyone who wants to know how the main tenures work, why there are still daunting housing problems, and whether the drastic changes now upon us will solve some of these problems or make matters worse.

There has been some misrepresentation and distortion of the real picture, especially in respect of what would constitute real freedom of choice in housing, and the cost to the public purse of the different tenures. All too often the case against misleading ideas has been allowed to go by default. If this guide makes a contribution towards showing how housing finance systems have worked, what has been wrong, and the direction which reform should take, it will have served its purpose.

Henry Aughton, November 1990

Council Housing

For practical purposes, council housing did not exist until the responsibility of acting as the main providers of future rented housing was placed on the local authorities by the Housing Act 1919. Until then, a handful of charitable trusts, forerunners of the housing association movement, had built more houses than all the councils put together.

This must have seemed a surprising choice. Councils had no experience in large scale housing provision. Other countries faced similar problems, but they turned to the housing association movement. That choice was not open to Britain, whose housing associations were too few, and too small, to be expected to deal effectively with the colossal tasks which this country faced in the aftermath of the first world war. The decision of the then coalition government, and every successive government until 1979, to place the responsibility for providing and managing rented housing on the local authorities, has been more than justified by their achievements.

Let us consider then, the way that councils operate as housing authorities, and the statutory and financial institutions which govern their actions.

Providing the houses

Houses are built on borrowed money. An individual buys or builds with the help of a loan, usually from a building society or a bank, paid back with interest over a period of probably 25 years. A council also finances the building of houses through loans, but repayment is over 60 years — the assumed life of a house.

Governments invariably set down the period within which any

loans raised by a council must be repaid. Councils can repay over a shorter period if they wish, but most go for the longest term available. They are anxious to keep annual loan charges (interest on the loans plus an element of repayment of the principal) down to a minimum.

Repayment was by what is called the sinking fund method, a formula which means a very small repayment of principal in the first year. In each year that follows, the sum to be repaid is worked out by adding five per cent to the previous year's payment. The starting point was calculated so that by the sixtieth year, the whole loan would have been repaid. Interest on the outstanding loan decreases a little each year, since it was payable on a declining amount. It was rather like the annuity method used with building society mortgage loans (unless these are of the endowment type); principal repayments gradually increase, interest payments gradually decline.

Capital expenditure

In providing houses, it is necessary to incur expenditure on land, roads, sewers, and of course, the buildings themselves. The expenditure on the acquisition of these permanent assets is called **capital expenditure** (as distinct from recurring annual expenditure such as running costs and loan charges, which is **revenue expenditure**). The transactions involved are recorded in a housing capital account, showing on the expenditure side what has been spent on land, roads, sewers, construction and preparation costs, and on the income side the loans raised to finance the operation and any capital receipts (from the sale of houses or land) which have been used to meet some of the expenditure. There may also be contributions from revenue, but these are likely to be small.

Where the loans come from

A council has many services besides housing which need loans to finance capital spending. Instead of letting each service raise its own loans, it has a Loans Fund, which raises money from financial institutions, the government's Public Works Loan Board, companies, and individuals. The Loans Fund acts as a lender to whichever department needs to borrow for capital spending. This is a great accounting and administrative convenience, and has other important advantages. The Loans Fund borrows most of its money for fixed terms of anything from two to sixty years. Only a small proportion of the Loan Fund requirements will be met by 'temporary' borrowing — money repayable at short notice — so unlike a building society there is no problem of rapid withdrawals of large amounts when interest rate changes make other forms of investment more attractive. The bulk of the money will have been borrowed for long periods at fixed rates of interest, and the average rate of interest on the total borrowings of any local authority will change only slightly each year. The method provides great stability.

The Loans Fund has to pay interest, of course, to all those from whom it has borrowed. It recharges this interest, at an average rate (called the loans pool rate) to all the services which owe it money. Each year, it gets back from each of the services, like housing, the interest on the loans and an appropriate amount of repayment of principal.

Government control of capital spending

It seems rather difficult to believe these days, but until 1976 there was no restriction on the number of houses any council chose to build, and no council ever used this freedom irresponsibly. Consent to borrow on each scheme, called a loan sanction, had to be sought, but as long as this complied with government guidelines on building costs, a loan sanction would not be refused. However, in 1976 there was a financial crisis, which provoked the need to seek an International Monetary Fund loan on terms which required a reduction in public expenditure. From then on, the government took control over the amount of housing that councils could provide, at first by the loan sanction process.

Loan sanctions disappeared in 1978. Instead, each council had to produce a Local Housing Strategy (LHS) setting out the need in its area for new council building and other housing projects. On the basis of this, it then had to draw up a Housing Investment Programme (HIP), showing what it planned to spend on the items covered by the strategy. The DoE then considered both and allocated borrowing permission for a total sum, instead of for individual items.

At first, the new HIP system was well received — it was a simpler method of cost control, and the commonsense of local strategy planning was obvious. But while councils were saved a lot of work, central government had acquired new and sweeping powers to control capital spending on housing which it began to use in an arbitrary and blundering fashion. HIP allocations were suddenly cut in June 1979, three months into the financial year. And in February 1980, a moratorium on spending was suddenly announced.

In the meantime, the Local Government Planning and Land Act 1980 created a further restriction by shifting control from *borrowing* to expenditure. Instead of a block allocation of borrowing permission, there was, from 1981-82 onwards, a block allocation of permitted capital *expenditure*.

There was another confusion. The sale of council houses from 1980 onwards was beginning to produce large capital receipts. Half of these were intended to be available as an addition to the HIP allocation. But until sales took place, councils had no idea how much extra this would allow them to spend. Investment fell further as they underestimated what they could spend. By the autumn of 1982, councils were being urged to spend more on council housing. It was, to say the least, a remarkable exercise in financial management.

This display of profligacy was short-lived. From April 1984, the proportion of capital receipts which could be used was reduced to 40 per cent (25 per cent in Wales), and reduced again to 20 per cent (15 per cent in Wales) in 1985. Central government control over the housing programme had increased enormously.

Revenue expenditure

When a scheme is built, capital expenditure ceases. From then on there will be continuing spending on management, repairs, loan charges and other items. This recurring expenditure is known as **revenue expenditure** and is met from the rents charged, housing subsidies (if any), interest on capital receipts and mortgage interest from the sale of council houses. (These two last items are described in more detail later). Until 1990, there could also be a contribution from the rates. This was compulsory if the housing revenue account would otherwise have been in deficit.

All these transactions were shown in a housing revenue account (HRA) which every housing authority had to keep in a form prescribed by the Department of the Environment. Since April 1990, this takes a very different form. For a comparison of the pre- and post-1990 HRAs, see below.

Table 1

Typical housing revenue account, pre—1990/91

Expenditure	£000s
Loan charges:	
principal	665
interest	4,221
Supervision and management:	
general	712
special	383
Repair and maintenance	2,208
Transfer to general rate fund	276
Other expenditure	83
Working balance at end of year	1,495
Total debits	10,043

Income	
Working balance at beginning of year	1,383
Net rent income	3,248
Rent rebates:	
to tenants on income support	1,853
all other cases	1,049
Heating and other amenity charges	49
Housing Act subsidy	5
Other rent income (not housing)	255
Miscellaneous income	433
Interest receivable	1,711
Rate fund contribution towards rebate costs	57
Total credits	10,043

Note: Total rent income consists of net rent income and the two rent rebates items. These are government grants reimbursing rebates granted to tenants.

Table 2

Typical housing revenue account, post 1990/91

Expenditure   **£000s**

Loan charges:		
	principal	578
	interest	2,804
Supervision and management:		
	general	753
	special	425
Repair and maintenance		2,550
Housing benefit		2,850
Other		60
Contingency		50
Working balance carried forward		864
Total debits		10,934

Income

Working balance brought forward		918
Rents:		
	dwellings	6,450
	other properties	318
HRA Subsidy		2,750
Interest on:		
	balances	180
	loans for house purchase	250
Other		68
Total credits		10,934

Notes: ◢ Housing benefit is rent rebates, treated as expenditure.
    ◢ Rents are the full rents before the granting of rebates.
    ◢ HRA subsidy replaces the former separate housing subsidy and
     rent rebate subsidy.

Rents

There were, inevitably, differences in council rent levels in different parts of the country, but these differences were greatly exaggerated by many commentators. Average rents for 1989 — 90 were estimated by CIPFA (the Chartered Institute of Public Finance and Accountancy) at:

▲ Greater London   £25.69 per week
▲ Metropolitan Districts   £19.93   "   "
▲ Non-Metropolitan Districts   £20.19   "   "

In the regions, the highest is Wales at £22.35, with all the rest varying between £21.90 in the South and £18.84 in East Anglia.

Not much difference there. But there were differences between one local authority and another within a region because of differing land and building costs when the houses were being built, and also because of the different attitudes of councils towards the amount of help that should be given by rate contributions. Even so, the comparative closeness of the average rents of most authorities in any region has been remarkable, especially when compared with the differing housing costs of homebuyers.

Rent pooling and rent fixing

Similarity in the rents of similar dwellings in a local authority area was achieved by rent pooling. The rents of each separate scheme used to be calculated as each was completed, taking into account annual costs on that scheme (loan charges, repairs and management), and any help with housing subsidy or rate fund contributions. So with different schemes of identical houses there were often significant differences in the rents charged. A few of the more progressive councils began to see that the simple solution was to do for the whole stock what they had been doing for each individual scheme — look at the outgoings in total, deduct total subsidies and rate fund contributions, and see what needed to be met by rent income.

Having settled what total income was needed, the council then had to decide what the rents of individual properties should be, so that the rent of any dwelling would be seen as fair when compared to others. Every dwelling was assessed for rating purposes for its gross value which was supposed to represent the annual rent which a landlord would expect to receive. Gross values provide a ready made basis of comparing one property with another, reflecting size, quality and location. Most councils used this system, or a refined formula of their own.

Where gross rating value was the chosen basis, all the council had to do was calculate net outgoings, say £15 million where expenditure and rate fund contributions produced that answer, and then look at the total gross value of all the houses. Say this was £10 million. Individual rents of one and a half times gross value would produce the required rent income of £15 million to keep the housing account in balance.

The acceptance of rent pooling spread, and became virtually universal in the years following the second world war, as the logic and convenience of the system was recognised. Central government realised that rent pooling transferred the benefit of subsidies on earlier built houses to the later ones which had cost so much more. It would dearly have liked to withdraw subsidies on earlier schemes but settled for taking the effect of rent pooling into account when future subsidy levels were introduced.

Councils listened to the exhortations of government to introduce rebates to help tenants who found even pooled rents a burden, and the number of locally operated schemes grew steadily but their effect was usually limited. Most councils felt that income support was a matter for government, not for them; their business was to provide houses at reasonable rents with the help of subsidies.

The rent pooling system of course, only applies within the area of each local authority. Neighbouring councils have differing average rent levels for reasons of historic accident, such as the proportion of earlier-built low cost houses or the size of the current building programme. The issue produced a lot of discussion in the 1970s and there were advocates of national rent pooling, but enthusiasm was lacking amongst councils which might lose slightly, and no government has shown any particular interest.

What are housing subsidies?

There have been two kinds of payment by the Exchequer which affect the housing revenue account. One has been housing subsidy under the Housing Acts, which meets part of housing costs with the

rates in 1989, councils found themselves charging 14.5 per cent on their mortgage loans, about 3-4 per cent more than is needed — average loans pool rates are mostly between 10 and 11 per cent. The damage and hardship which the system inflicts on those who chose a council mortgage, usually the less well off purchasers, is manifest.

Financial effects of sales

If a sale is financed by a council mortgage loan, the council makes a saving on repairs costs, perhaps some saving on management costs, and receives interest on the outstanding loan. Against this it loses the rent and any housing subsidy payable.

There will also be an annual repayment of principal, very little in the early years, more in later years. But since this is a capital receipt it will not be credited to the housing revenue account. It will be applied to reducing the council's housing debt, or be added to other housing capital receipts and used for capital spending, or be invested.

Most sales, however, will be financed from some other source, probably a building society. As with a council loan there will be savings on repairs and perhaps management, and there will be a loss of rent income and subsidy where this was still payable. But because the council receives the whole of the sale price at once, there will be no annual mortgage repayments.

If the proceeds are invested, there will be investment income, and this goes to the income side of the housing revenue account. If they are used for debt redemption, the loan charges falling on the HRA will be less. And if they are used for new capital expenditure, the HRA will benefit by having less loan charges to bear than if the council had borrowed to finance that capital expenditure.

Other effects of council house sales

There is no doubt about the advantages of the right to buy scheme for those who can afford to buy. For the council, however, the advantages of sales are a matter of some controversy. The selling price, even after the huge discount, will generally be much more than the outstanding debt on the house, and it has therefore been argued that selling cannot fail to be profitable. This is like saying that someone who sells a house worth £50,000, bought long ago for £10,000 and with an outstanding mortgage loan of say £6,000, gains £14,000 by selling for £20,000 (£20,000 proceeds less outstanding loan £6,000, net proceeds £14,000). This is obvious nonsense. An asset worth £50,000 has been exchanged for £20,000 cash. The net proceeds are £14,000 when they ought to be £44,000.

There are two even more important issues. First, there is the elementary question as to what sense there can be in selling houses so far below their real value that it will take several sales to provide one replacement of similar quality; and this at a time of such desperate scarcity of rented accommodation.

Second, the alleged profitability of such sales is an illusion. The immediate apparent gain — investment income on sale proceeds which exceeds rent income — is real enough the first year, but is less the year after by the amount by which the rent would have risen if the house had been retained. And less again the year after, and in a few years a cross-over point is reached and the gains turn into losses of ever greater magnitude.

A financial appraisal of the effects of sales was in fact produced for the Labour government in 1977, but not published. It came to light only because of its disclosure by The Guardian's correspondent David Hencke some years later. It showed sales as resulting in profits to councils in the earlier years, as mortgage repayments exceeded what the rents would have been, turning into substantial losses in later years as rents continued to increase. A second paper, done for the new Conservative government in 1980 (presumably by the same civil servants, with admirable flexibility of mind) showed continuing profits. The different answer resulted from the different assumptions made in the second paper about future subsidies, costs, and rent increases.

A study, carried out for the House of Commons Environment Select Committee and published in 1981, found that some of the assumptions which enabled the second paper to portray sales as yielding a profit were totally unrealistic. It calculated that, in fact, the long term losses on council house sales, calculated over a 50 year period, were likely to average £12,500 per dwelling. On this basis the million houses sold so far mean an eventual loss of £12,500 million (at mid-1980s prices). Yet even these calculations did not allow for the enormous rent increases which have actually occurred since 1981.

This has been a disgraceful episode, and the lack of interest shown in it by the press, and worse still, the Opposition, is inexplicable.

Another sleight of hand by the DoE was its claim that it would generously allow councils to supplement their HIP allocations and so increase the amount they could spend on housing provision or improvement, by letting them use part of the capital receipts which come from sales for capital spending. At first the DoE said 50 per cent, then 40 per cent, then 20 per cent. This dishonesty — for that was what it was — again went unchallenged on the main count, which is that until 1980, councils had always had the undisputed right to use the full proceeds of the sale of any capital asset so long as they used it for other capital purposes.

Restrictions on the use of capital receipts in the 1980s resulted in a huge accumulation of receipts in local authority coffers, reaching £6 billion in the late 1980s. Meanwhile authorities saw their HIP allocations reduced year after year as the condition of their housing stocks declined. The money was there to tackle the problems of disrepair and modernisation, but the government made it even more difficult to spend. The Local Government and Housing Act 1989 required authorities to use receipts to write off old debts rather than invest in better housing. This is discussed later.

Council housing after 1989

When the Conservatives won the 1987 election they could look back on the great strides they had made. Over a million council houses had passed into owner-occupation. Council building for rent had reduced sharply to an appalling 16,111 starts in 1988, while a million families remained on council waiting lists. Housing subsidies, £1,423 million in 1980-81, had been cut to £409 million in 1985-86. And those changes to the subsidy system resulted in massive rent increases, as intended.

But in the government's view, much still remained to be done, and a White Paper, Housing: The Government's proposals (Cm 214, September 1987), set out the next aims.

The proportion of owner-occupation in Britain, one of the highest in the world, was to be expanded. Housing associations, together with private and commercial landlords, were to be the future providers of rented housing. Private landlords would have freedom to charge market rents for new lettings.

Council housing still dominated the rented market; but in the government's view it was often not in the best interests of tenants. Although management was good in some places, it was distant and bureaucratic in the big cities, with poor maintenance performance in many areas. There was indiscriminate subsidy from the rates; and whole communities had slipped into permanent dependency on the welfare state. Local authorities should therefore cease to provide housing, and would have an 'enabling' role in encouraging other landlords to make provision.

The White Paper said that council tenants must have more opportunity to control their own destinies, including the right to choose other landlords. There were to be powers to set up housing action trusts to renovate run-down council housing in the inner cities.

These changes required a reform of housing finance, set out in two consultation papers issued in July 1988. One was called *Capital expenditure and finance* and covered other services as well as housing; the other, *New financial regime for local authority housing*, dealt with the housing revenue account, subsidies, rents and housing finance generally.

The proposals in the White Paper were introduced in the Housing Act 1988. The financial reforms followed in the Local Government and Housing Act 1989, which came into force on 1 April 1990.

The new capital finance system

The system in operation until April 1990 controlled the capital *expenditure* of councils and prescribed what this was: mainly acquisition and development of land, building work, vehicles, plant and machinery, housing repairs when the cost is met by borrowing, and capital grants and advances. Expenditure was authorised by the annual Housing Investment Programme (HIP), and the allocation was normally backed by borrowing approval. Repair work not financed by borrowing did not count as 'prescribed expenditure'.

There was a ten per cent tolerance between years to allow for the carry-over of unspent allocations. Overspending was not illegal.

Capital receipts (mainly from the sale of council houses) could also be used, though only 20 per cent of the amount available could be carried forward for use in later years, or could be applied to 'non-prescribed' expenditure. This facility, known as 'the cascade', was widely used to meet major repair costs without having to borrow (which would have used up scarce borrowing permission). The right to carry forward unspent capital receipts was seen by housing authorities as natural. It was their money, arising from the sale of their property. But the government saw the 'cascade effect' as a danger. Apparently it had not occurred to it that one result of restricting the use of capital receipts would be that the unspent balance would build up.

The new system therefore sets out to control *borrowing*, instead of *expenditure*. It applies to the financing of any capital expenditure not met from revenue.

The definition of what constitutes capital expenditure is wider than before. For example, it includes 'enhancement' which is anything that substantially lengthens the life of an asset, increases its market value, or increases the extent to which it can be used.

Each year the DoE issues to each council its HIP allocation, specifying what capital expenditure is authorised, and what capital receipts will be taken into account when fixing borrowing limits. These will be set by a basic credit approval (BCA), and perhaps supplementary credit approvals (SCA).

There is a fundamental change to the rules for the use of capital receipts. Only 25 per cent of receipts can be used for capital purposes. The remaining 75 per cent must be used to repay debt, despite the fact that councils face gigantic problems of repair and modernisation, and even though their housing debt is a tiny fraction of the current value of their property. There is about as much sense in this as there would be if a householder, faced with a leaking roof, were to use all his or her available cash to make a premature reduction in their outstanding mortgage.

Each council is issued with a basic credit approval (BCA) for the coming year. This is the council's authority to meet capital expenditure by borrowing or credit arrangements. In fixing the BCA, the secretary of state can take account of the usable capital receipts belonging to that council. The BCA covers all council services, but the housing element in it is stated as the loan charges which are eligible for Housing Revenue Account Subsidy. It can only be used in the year to which it relates. Any unused allocation cannot be carried forward, and any overspending will be deducted from the following year's BCA.

There is no limit on the amount of capital expenditure which can be charged to revenue, but the freedom is more cosmetic than actual. Any use of it will affect rent levels, since no support can be given from the general fund.

Supplementary credit approvals (SCA) may be issued at any time. Approvals for estate action schemes and the use of the special homelessness money available in 1990/91 (see p 38) are the sort of items which SCAs will cover.

Under the previous system, grants made by the housing authority for renovation or improvement were financed by borrowing, with the council receiving annual government subsidy towards the cost of the loan charges on such borrowing. In future, subsidy will be by a lump sum grant called a specified capital grant.

Leasing arrangements on property, plant, vehicles and other items, widely used by councils in recent years, are now brought within the new capital system. They must be taken into account when a council's aggregate credit limit (ACL) is calculated. This broadly consists of outstanding debt plus the council's credit arrangements. A council has no power to borrow if it would cause the ACL to be exceeded. The extent of 'credit cover' deemed to be used when a credit arrangement is entered into will be the cost in the first and subsequent years, discounted by a formula determined by the secretary of state.

Besides all the new constraints listed above, any borrowing must be from British-based lenders, unless there is consent to do otherwise.

The new housing revenue system

Ninety-five councils still received £483 million housing subsidy in 1987-88, and all councils received rent rebate subsidy which met almost the total cost of rent rebates. Some councils who were not getting housing subsidy, were nevertheless giving substantial help to the HRA from the rates. Others, who were receiving housing subsidy, were producing surpluses which they transferred to their general rate funds. And some managed to balance their HRAs with rate fund contributions totalling £115 million less than the assessments on which they were receiving rate support grant.

In addition, the financial arrangements had failed to cope with changing circumstances. Because councils borrow on a historic cost basis, the cost of borrowing is eroded by inflation. This applies to house purchasers too, or anyone else who borrows in inflationary times. As a result, there was a growing tendency towards bigger surpluses in HRAs. The government concluded that, since the effect of new building by councils has been partly offset by surpluses on earlier, low-cost building, less new building in future by councils meant that the benefit of the earlier building was even greater.

It therefore believed that these surpluses should not be available as a cushion for bad practice and inefficiency. While rents should not exceed levels within the reach of people in low paid employment, and in practice will frequently be below market levels, the government wanted them set by reference to two parameters — what people can pay and what the property is worth — rather than by reference to historic cost.

Fundamental to the new system is a new style housing revenue account. The figures on page 18 show the main changes.

Rent increases

Since 1981-1982, the government had been making assumptions about the rent increases which it expected every council to make. Annual 'guideline' increase fluctuated between 60p and £2.95 per

week, for no very clear reason. The guideline increase was the same figure for every council, north or south, urban or rural, irrespective of the state of the HRA. It was left to each council to decide how to treat individual dwellings and compliance with government wishes was not universal.

Under the new system, with the need to move towards rents which, while having regard to what people can pay, are also related to what the property is worth, each authority's average rent increase is calculated individually. This involves assessing the capital value of the housing stock of each council, using right to buy sale values (before discount). From this, the total value of all housing stock in the country is derived. Each authority's stock is expressed as a proportion of the total national value, and the government then decides what overall *national* increase it wants to see for the relevant year.

The next step is to calculate how much each authority's share should be. This is the same proportion of the national increase as the council's share of the national capital value. This is expressed as an amount per dwelling, per week.

It should be noted that, in doing this, the DoE is not using capital values as the basis for rent *levels* (as the Duke of Edinburgh's report recommended in 1985), but for determining the amount of rent *increase*, regardless of current rent levels. It is an odd way of doing things, and with the vast difference in house prices across the country, the arithmetic produced some odd results. For example, Hillingdon would need rents averaging £39.39, which means an increase of 65 per cent. But Blackburn rents should be £10.74, a reduction of 51 per cent.

The assumed increases have therefore been subjected to a 'damping' process, so that changes are not excessive in any year. For 1990-91, this produced maximum guideline increases of £4.50 a week, with a minimum of 95p. Sixty-six authorities, mainly in London and the South East, come out at the maximum level of £4.50, and 170, mainly in the Midlands and the North at the minimum, 95p. The rest are somewhere in between.

That £4.50 maximum was a very large increase, since £2.95 had been the highest 'guideline' figure in the preceding eight years. But the new financial regime also allowed authorities to increase rents even further. The London borough of Redbridge increased rents by £15.64 a week (a 44 per cent increase) instead of the guideline 95p; Canterbury £12.29, (guideline £1.92), a 54 per cent increase; Bournemouth £9.00, guideline £1.32, a 33 per cent increase.

32

There has been no report of any DoE disapproval of these outrageous increases. Indeed, the experience of West Oxfordshire, a council under Conservative control, seems to indicate the DoE's total indifference to or even approval of this issue. West Oxfordshire found itself obliged to impose a 75 per cent increase, £7.15 a week, instead of 95p. This was because of the way the new HRA subsidy worked in their case. The DoE, replying to the council's protest, said that it considered the increase to be acceptable, as tenants 'are still subsidised because the rent is based on the historic cost of the dwelling'. It is not easy to understand the mentality that can produce such an answer.

Management and maintenance

The new system requires the DoE, when devising a notional HRA for each council, to make assumptions about management and maintenance expenditure. It assumed an eight per cent increase for 1990-91 — five per cent for inflation and three per cent real increase to allow for something for the backlog of repairs. As councils had found it necessary to increase spending by 10.25 per cent in 1989-90, and costs were still rising, they felt that the eight per cent was not enough. To make matters worse, the previous widespread practice of borrowing or using capital receipts to meet the cost of major repairs will suffer serious restriction under the new capital system. The choice is therefore to cut repairs programmes, or further increase rents.

The assumed eight per cent increase for 1990-91 was a total for the whole country. Allocations to individual councils took account of average expenditure over three previous years, with an allowance for inflation. There was also an attempt to bring some of the lowest spending authorities up to a certain minimum level. Again, some wide variations have resulted — Camden is allowed £1,490 per dwelling, Islington £965, Stockport £765, Wigan £577.

For future years the DoE intends to assess more closely the spending needs of each authority, and further changes will follow.

The reasons for change

Most of the criticisms of the old system are too superficial to be accepted as justification for the sweeping changes that have been made. It is useful to look at what most commentators believe were the *real* reasons.

The 1980 subsidy system produced massive rent increases which allowed housing subsidies to be reduced. They were £1,423m in 1980-81, and down to £298m by 1983-84, though they rose again in the following years to around £500m. Still, the saving of some £900m by the DoE looked quite an achievement.

Unfortunately, higher rents mean higher rebates, and more of them. Comparisons are difficult before 1983/84 because of changes in presentation and in the system, but from 1983/84 to 1988/89, rent rebate subsidy increased from £1,980m to £2,725m, an increase of £745m, and it was estimated to go on rising by an extra £300m a year thereafter. The cost to the Department of Social Security is more than the saving to the DoE. So, as a cost saving exercise, the 1980 Act was less than satisfactory.

Yet it was an article of faith with the government that council rents *must* go on increasing. But as higher rents allowed housing subsidies to be cut to a point where most authorities outside London no longer received them, the DoE lost its principal means for enforcing further increases. Not only that, some local authorities took their responsibilities to their constituents seriously, and considered that they were better placed than central government to assess local need.

For 70 years (apart from a brief interval in 1972-74), all governments had accepted that rent levels were a matter for the local authority, and with this went the right to give such financial support from the rates as it believed necessary. The DoE complained that many local councils did not manage their housing service effectively; but it also complained that some, still entitled to housing subsidy on DoE criteria, were actually managing things so well that they produced surpluses on their HRAs, and made contributions to the rate fund. Others, receiving rate support grant on their *assumed* need to make rate fund contributions to the HRA, made smaller contributions than their assessment indicated. The DoE felt aggrieved. Most councils, however, felt that this was what local democracy, autonomy and accountability meant.

There was also the problem of rent rebate subsidy which increased steadily. Rent rebates are income support, a social security function, the cost of which has been properly charged to the social security programme, not to the housing programme. It was a cost to be borne by the taxpayer, the community at large, just like the cost of rent allowances which help the tenants of housing associations and private landlords. This rent rebate subsidy provided automatic reimbursement of over 90 per cent of the cost of rebates. The cost, it seemed, was unavoidable, and it would go on increasing. The Treasury observed all this with a jaundiced eye.

Changes had to be made which would restore the DoE's leverage for enforcing rent increases, reduce the power of local councils to give rate aid, and above all, reduce the burden on the Exchequer of the cost of rent rebates.

How the changes work

The new arrangements mean a massive transfer of power to central government of virtually all meaningful decisions about council housing — on rent levels, on expenditure on maintenance, improvement and rehabilitation, and on management.

This is mainly secured by two major changes. The first is the new form of HRA, with gross rents the dominating item on the income side, and rent rebates as expenditure instead of, as previously, as an income item.

The second major change is the new HRA subsidy to replace housing subsidy (where it was still payable), rent rebate subsidy (which every council received), and rate fund contributions. It is a deficiency subsidy, not on the actual HRA, but on a notional HRA produced by the DoE for every housing authority as described earlier.

By abolishing rent rebate subsidy, the DoE ensures that every housing authority, at least for the present, will need HRA subsidy. This means that every authority will be subject to DoE control on rent levels. The DoE points out, however, that councils will have complete freedom to determine rents; and this is true, so long as they produce the specified rent income. Indeed, they will even have freedom to set rents which produce less than the specified rent income; so long as they reduce expenditure which offsets the reduced rent income.

It is the same with expenditure. Councils are free to spend above DoE criteria; as long as they increase rents still further, to cover the overspending. If there is a deficit, this must be carried forward and budgeted for, in the following year.

Looking ahead, the DoE points out that councils enjoy the benefit of loan charges based on historic cost. As rents continue to rise, loan charges will not increase, since there will be little new capital expenditure financed by borrowing, and 75 per cent of capital receipts will be going to debt redemption. It follows that deficiencies, and therefore HRA subsidy, will decrease.

The DoE will be able to say, hand on heart, that increasing income reduces the need for support from public funds; and there is, of course, a responsibility to keep the call on the public purse to a minimum. It expects that a number of councils will quickly reach the point where they will no longer need HRA subsidy, and are producing surpluses. As that happy stage is reached, the DoE will direct the council to transfer a prescribed amount to its general fund, reducing the call on the poll tax payer. Or, alternatively, it could reduce the amount of revenue support grant (formerly the rate support grant); and that, too, will help the poll taxpayer. The number of authorities that reach this position will grow steadily as time goes on.

To speed this up, the DoE will doubtless feel obliged to steadily

increase its intervention into all aspects of council housing policy and management, bringing an increase in centralisation and a decrease in local responsibility beyond anything we have seen in our lifetime.

To secure these objectives, the DoE needs massive rent increases, and the strategy for obtaining these is the declared policy of 'what people can pay and what the property is worth' for rent fixing. There have been many references to 'affordability' but a notable absence of definitions of what this means. It looks as if relationship to current property values, rather than affordability, is going to be the main consideration.

Workers in service industries, pensioners, people with low incomes generally, usually have earnings based on national scales; and when they do not, their incomes will certainly bear little relationship to the huge variations in property prices in different areas. For these people, who make up the bulk of council tenants, council housing, with its minimal variations in rent levels in the various regions, has been a blessing. The South East region, the most expensive in England, had unrebated rents in 1988-89 which averaged £21.30. The least expensive were East Anglia (£18.84) and Yorkshire and Humberside (£18.85). The rest were in between. (CIPFA Rent Statistics at April 1989).

But average house prices varied between £81,184 in the South East and £30,707 in the North. (*Housing Finance* no.3, Council of Mortgage Lenders, 1989,). What possible justification can there be for attempting to relate rent levels to this? And if we do, what becomes of labour mobility?

All this arises from the absurd ideological dogma which argues that unless rents represent a return on current values, the tenant is being subsidised even if he or she is paying more than the cost of providing and maintaining the accommodation.

This selective vision ignores the subsidising of house purchase by mortgage interest tax relief — that remarkable system which gives help whether there is need or not, and subsidises at a higher rate if the mortgagor is in a higher tax bracket.

Yet the government seems set on its course, and the outlook in the coming years is that council rents will go on rising steeply, the proportion of tenants who need rebates will rise further, and the cost of rebates will rise spectacularly. The government will then find itself attempting to shift that large and growing burden onto a diminishing proportion of tenants who are not eligible for rebates.

This particular exercise is the most discreditable of these 'reforms'. There is no intention of treating housing associations in this fashion, and even to think of trying to do so to private landlords would be ludicrous.

Meanwhile, waiting lists will lengthen, and the scandal and economic folly of homelessness will go on increasing, for nothing effective is proposed to deal with the basic cause — the shortage of rented accommodation.

The costs of homelessness

It is impossible to be precise about the costs of homelessness. How can a monetary value be placed on broken relationships, ruined childhoods and lost job opportunities? In terms of public expenditure, in a sense all the money spent by councils and most of that spent by housing associations on the provision of homes is about the prevention or relief of homelessness.

However, homelessness is only one factor, and a relatively minor one at that, in the formula used by the DoE to distribute capital spending allocations. In November 1989 the secretary of state announced a two year package of £250 million for additional help for the homeless, although conditions attached to the deal made it clear that councils had to channel resources into housing association provision, and that they themselves were not going to be able to build new houses.

This package followed a period during which homelessness had been increasing rapidly and the government had appeared to be uninterested in the problem. The 1987 White Paper on housing failed to mention homelessness, yet between 1979 and 1990 there was a 122 per cent increase in the numbers of homeless households accepted by local authorities. The total for England and Wales in 1989-90 was no fewer than 137,000.

By 1990, the government's concern had grown to the extent of two further measures to try to reduce the visible presence of the homeless on the street. The first was a trebling (to £2 million) in the support given to voluntary housing aid and advice agencies and the second was the announcement in June 1990 of £15 million for direct-access accommodation aimed at single homeless people.

These sums are dwarfed by the amounts spent each year by local authorities in providing for homeless people under the terms of Part 111 of the Housing Act, 1985. In the 1988-89 CIPFA statistics (based on only 314 authorities in England and Wales), total expenditure on the

the homeless was £68.187 million, of which £39.287 million (57.6 per cent) was spent by London councils.

Almost half of this total sum, £33 million, was spent on bed and breakfast accommodation. Hotels, of course, are both highly unsatisfactory for homeless people, and hugely expensive for local councils. The latest available figures, presented by the minister for the environment, David Trippier, in the House of Commons in 1989 suggest that the cost of keeping a family in bed and breakfast in London for a year is £14,600, but the first year of rehousing them into a new council house would only be £8,200. Outside London the comparison is less dramatic, but the figures nevertheless speak for themselves.

2 Housing Associations

Long before councils became involved in the provision of rented housing, there were housing associations, usually established with the aid of charitable money from wealthy benefactors, providing dwellings at modest rents. The Peabody, Guinness, and Sutton Dwelling Trust are three well-known examples.

The movement spread and eventually government subsidies similar to those paid to councils became available. New kinds of organisations were tried — cost-rent, co-ownership, co-operative, self-build; but by far the major provision was still of dwellings for rent for those in need. However, the total stock, some 250,000 dwellings by 1970, was still small compared to the five million or so then provided by councils.

The 1970-74 Conservative government decided upon a great expansion of the housing association movement as a supplement (or perhaps as an alternative) to council housing. The Housing Corporation, already set up in 1964 to encourage the formation of cost-rent and co-ownership societies, was chosen as the main agent for encouraging the formation of housing associations to provide accommodation at fair rents. The Corporation would have an important supervisory function; it would examine and approve schemes, and the government would provide the necessary financial support.

A Bill to provide the relevant powers was drafted, but before it reached the statute book, the 1974 Labour government had come into office. It promptly took over the previous government's measure without alteration. With the Housing Act 1974, the great expansion began.

The movement had already been growing and Shelter had played a notable part in that growth, raising some £3 million by national appeals in 1969 and 1970, which it used mainly to start housing associations in area of severe housing stress, and so supplement the work of the local authorities. By 1971, the associations were providing an extra 10,000 dwellings a year, a big increase on anything they had managed previously. But with the impetus given by the financial arrangements of the 1974 Act and the work of the Housing Corporation, this more than trebled by 1976, with 35,300 completions. Since then, however, there have been the dramatic cuts in public expenditure and some diversion of resources to conversion for sale. Annual completions have not been over 20,000 since 1980, and by 1987 had fallen to 11,898.

Yet the associations have widened the choice open to would-be tenants and this has been especially important because of their willingness to house groups who have, in the past, been excluded from council accommodation. It has to be admitted that councils have often had an understandable, but possibly excessive, preference for 'looking after their own'.

Finance for the great expansion

The dramatic progress from 1974 onwards resulted from a new subsidy system, though the word 'subsidy' was tactfully avoided. From then on it was 'capital grants' or housing association grants

(HAG). Previously, when subsidies were given, they had been annual ones, as in the local authority sector, to meet part of the running costs. Now they were once-for-all lump sum grants which met most of the capital cost immediately. With these went a new rent system, 'fair rents' set by rent officers, as in the private sector.

The starting point for the new system was the rent which the rent officer recommended. The likely annual costs of management and maintenance, which would be the first call on the rent income, were then estimated. What was left after meeting those costs would be available for meeting loan charges on any money borrowed. It would not be very much and would service a loan which would meet only a small proportion of the total capital cost of providing the dwellings. The rest, the major part of the capital cost, was met by an outright capital grant (HAG).

Suppose, for example, that the total cost of provision for a house outside London was £10,000 in 1975:

Table 3

How HAG was calculated, pre-1989	
	£
Fair rent £9 per week, per annum	470
Management and maintenance	150
Available to service loan raised	£ 320
This would cover loan charges on a loan of approximately	2,320
Housing association grant (HAG) would be	7,680
	£10,000

The grant in this example meant a payment of about 77 per cent of the total cost of provision, remarkably generous compared with previous systems. The associations were scarcely able to believe their good fortune. But this special treatment was needed for associations to expand, since they did not have the great advantage which councils had, of a large stock of earlier built low-cost housing which, by rent pooling, kept average rent levels down.

The enthusiasm of many councils for the new scheme was limited, as they compared it with their own subsidy scheme but they welcomed the greater variety and freedom of choice for tenants. The enthusiasm of the Treasury was likewise restrained, for the immediate cost was very heavy. Yet that large once-for-all subsidy in 1975, £7,680 in the example quoted, had produced a dwelling which must now be worth over £50,000, with a mere £2,000 or so outstanding loan debt. A remarkable bargain, by any standards.

Of course, by 1989 there had been a dramatic change. The rent which a rent officer would set had trebled, and the cost of provision had more than trebled. Inevitably, the cost of subsidising had risen steeply, to 80 or 90 per cent of a much higher cost of provision, hence the government's growiing concern and the new financial arrangements from April 1989, described later.

There was a minor problem which the new system got over without difficulty. Development and other preliminary costs — land purchase, payments to the builder — have to be met before the rents begin to come in or the grant is finally settled. The Housing Corporation resolved this by providing temporary loans, the interest on which was treated as part of the overall cost of provision.

There could also be a second subsidy, a 'revenue deficit grant'. In the first year especially, rent income might not cover all the expenditure, and an association could find itself in deficit on its revenue account. Indeed, this situation might continue for a while if running costs turned out to be more than was allowed for in the grant calculation. A case could then be made to the DoE for grant assistance on the year's operations. The grant would not be a continuing one unless the need could be shown to persist.

There was one astonishing oversight in the 1974 Act. We live in inflationary times, and rents rise significantly at regular intervals. A capital grant (HAG) which was appropriate when the grant was given would be too generous for the circumstances a few years later when the rents had gone up substantially after several rent reviews. A scheme which broke even at first would soon be making a surplus. Yet the subsidy had all been given in one lump sum. It could not, like an annual subsidy, be reduced in future years when the need was less.

The light eventually dawned on the DoE, and the Housing Act 1980 required associations to keep a 'grant redemption fund' (GRF) into which surpluses on HAG-aided schemes were paid. The DoE could thus get some of its money back, or require surpluses to be used, for instance, for major repairs which otherwise would require grant aid.

Rents before the 1988 Act

The fair rents which housing associations charged as a condition of receiving HAG have been higher than for comparable council dwellings. The difference narrowed as the 1980 Act produced drastic rent increases for council housing but widened again as council rent increases slowed down as housing subsidies were reduced year after year until they ceased altogether for most councils outside London. As this happened the DoE lost much of its leverage for forcing rent increases on unwilling councils, and in the meantime, fair rents were continuing their uninterrupted upward course (see Table 4).

Sales

The 'right to buy' scheme under the Housing Act 1980, as it applies to council tenants, is described in the chapter on council housing. The government wanted to extend the scheme to housing associations but they objected strongly. They saw no justification for being compelled to sell off their stock when their very reason for existence was to own houses which could be let at modest rents. Most associations were registered charities which raised legal and moral problems with sales. The House of Lords agreed with this and the government gave way. It settled for giving the associations power to sell only if they so chose. Even then, the power would not apply where it was in conflict with the terms of an association's trust. Where associations did sell, the discounts were the same as for council dwellings sold.

Between 1980 and 1984, only 5,309 association houses were sold, about one per cent of the total stock. (In the same period council house sales were 625,775, about ten per cent of the stock).

The government tried again. The Housing and Building Control Act 1984 proposed to extend the sales scheme to all dwellings owned by charitable housing associations. Again, some pressure in the Commons, and very considerable pressure in the Lords, obliged the government to drop the proposal.

Table 4

Council rents versus fair rents

	Average council rents, England and Wales	Average fair rent for housing associations	% difference
	£	£	%
1978	5.85	10.08	72.3
1979	6.40	10.69	67.0
1980	7.71	12.52	62.4
1981	11.43	13.96	22.1
1982	13.50	15.62	15.7
1983	14.00	17.15	22.5
1984	14.71	18.65	26.8
1985	15.59	19.69	26.3
1986	16.41	21.42	30.5
1987	17.24	22.85	32.5
1988	18.74	24.75	32.1
1989	20.64	26.65	29.1

Source: Housing and Construction Statistics 1977-87 and 1990, Department of the Environment, and CIPFA Council Rents at April 1989

Instead it introduced a scheme for portable discounts called HOTCHA (Home-Ownership for Tenants of Charitable Housing Associations). Tenants whose association refused to agree a voluntary sale at a discount could apply for a grant equivalent to what the discount would have been if the association had been willing to sell. The grant had to be used to assist the purchase of a house on the open market. Only associations nominated by the Housing Corporation could operate the scheme, and in its first year only 31 associations (out of over 2,000) were nominated, and only 159 actual sales were completed.

It picked up the following year, with 2,599 sales, still a very modest figure compared with what was happening in the council sector. This is partly because unlike the council scheme, HOTCHA meant that the

Housing Corporation had to actually produce the money when the portable discount was awarded to the aspiring house purchaser. It therefore has to decide how much it would authorise each year by way of grants, and once this was taken up, no more was available that year. Tenants whose applications had not been met had to re-apply the following year.

Those councils who had been admonished for taking too much time with *right to buy* watched this performance with the HOTCHA scheme with mild amusement. The government has now introduced a new system to replace HOTCHA, but the intention of the new Tenants Incentive Scheme (TIS) is the same — spreading home-ownership.

The Housing Act 1988

In its 1987 White Paper, the government saw the housing association movement as the standard bearer for the provision of rented housing. Councils would be 'enablers', not providers; future provision would be the task of housing associations and private landlords (described as 'the independent rented sector').

This future provision was to be funded by a much higher element of private finance. However, the associations had been heavily dependent on Exchequer support, typically capital grants of 80-90 per cent of the cost of provision because fair rents had covered only a small proportion of their costs. So assured tenancies will be required when associations provide new dwellings, or re-let existing dwellings, to allow them to charge higher rents to service privately-raised loans.

The legal framework for the new arrangements was provided in the Housing Act 1988. Since changes in the grant structure do not require legislation (the secretary of state has the necessary powers) the provisions of the Act, insofar as they affect housing associations, dealt with the introduction of assured and assured shorthold forms of tenancy, security of tenure, rights of succession, and other matters which arise from the changeover from the fair rents system. The Housing Corporation continues to supervise associations in England. It has wide powers to determine grant levels and procedures. New bodies, Tai Cymru (Housing for Wales), and Scottish Homes (a merger of the Scottish Special Housing Association and the Housing Corporation in Scotland) have taken on the Housing Corporation's responsibilities there.

The new regime

From 1 April 1989, there have been far-reaching changes to virtually all the arrangements for providing future housing association dwellings and the financial management of the existing stock.

The new system is based on the premise that the more private finance that is available, the greater will be the provision of rented housing, as limited public finance will be stretched further.

The new system, therefore, provides that although HAG will continue to be available, its average proportion of the cost of new build or rehabilitation will be less than before. The remaining amount which needs to be borrowed (and which all used to count as public expenditure because it came from the Housing Corporation or the local authority), will in future mostly be provided from private finance under 'mixed funding' arrangements.

Under the old HAG system, the amount of grant depended on what the fair rent would be and the cost of each individual scheme. The government's solution is to reverse the procedure by taking the cost of provision as the starting point, and avoiding the considerable amount of detailed work that used to fall on the Housing Corporation by assessing grant rates based on tables of costs in eight geographical areas, for ten different sizes of dwelling and for four categories of provision — new build, rehabilitation, and two groups of special provision. For example, the all-in cost of an 80 square metre three to five person dwelling in Group A (the most expensive) is £120,000; in Group G (the cheapest) it is £50,000.

The overall average level of grants is said to be 75 per cent (against 80 to 90 per cent under the old HAG). The apparent lack of adequate consideration in the early stages is surprising. At first there was talk of 30 per cent public, 70 per cent private funding, to produce twice or three times as many houses as under the old system. There was a change of mind, as it was realised what this would mean in terms of rent levels, and a 50/50 sharing was indicated. Finally, in December 1988, as the consequences of a 50/50 system dawned, it was announced that there would be a public funding average of 75 per cent, with no upper limit. One is reminded of Wilde's Lady Bracknell: to have to do one's sums twice may be regarded as a misfortune; to have to do them a third time looks like carelessness.

The funding framework

There are now two main types of funding — 'mixed', with HAG from public sources, and the rest raised from private sources; and 'public' where HAG comes from the Housing Corporation and the rest, the loans, comes either from the Housing Corporation or the local authority.

Associations capable of raising private loans must do so. Many will be too small or not able for other reasons to do this and will have to look, as before, to the local council or the Housing Corporation.

The financing of developments is also divided into three other groups, 'tariff', 'non-tariff mixed funding' and 'non-tariff public funding'. Tariff funding is for financially strong associations. They will submit a three year programme of development, not individual scheme applications. The 'tariff' is a cash sum per dwelling, and the association will negotiate a tariff agreement with each regional office of the Housing Corporation in whose area it proposes to build housing. The agreement will define areas, housing need, numbers and types of dwellings, and the grant payable during the three years. Once set, the tariff will not be amended. There will be no individual scheme scrutiny. Mixed funding will apply.

Non-tariff mixed funding is for associations which are expected to use mixed funding, but are not suitable in terms of size, reserves and so on, for tariff funding. There will be assessment of individual schemes. There will also be some limited allowance for cost variation after approval. Costs usually rise while the work is under way, so this can be allowed for at the final assessment. There is less risk here for an association than in tariff funding but any excess cost over the above limit will have to be met by the association.

Non-tariff public funding applies to associations unlikely to attract private finance such as those catering for special needs or providing hostels. The procedure is the same as for non-tariff mixed funding, apart from some additional scrutiny at project approval stage to cover planning, land valuation and minor matters.

'Affordable' rents

For properties provided under the new regime; associations are expected to set rents which will cover costs while still being affordable for tenants on low incomes. Affordability, which is the term used by the government, is of course a problem for the associations because of the lack of definition. As a general guide the National Federation of Housing Associations has produced a table of 'indicative rents' for all the ten sizes of dwelling and all the geographical areas for which the cost tables cater. They range, for example, from £37.40 a week for an 80 square metre, three to five person house in area A (the most costly) to £26.50 in area G (the least costly).

The figures will be updated annually. They are an attempt to relate affordability to 20 per cent of tenants' average net incomes (i.e. earnings less tax and national insurance).

For existing tenancies, these will continue to be secure with fair rents set by the rent officer which will increase as they are re-registered every two years.

Re-lets of existing properties will be assured tenancies with the association, not the rent officer, fixing the rents. They, like the fair rents of existing tenants, may be eligible for revenue deficit grant (RDG) if necessary, and both groups will be subject to the new rules of the rent surplus fund (RSF) described later.

The DoE has indicated that while on re-let rents should remain within reach of the lower paid, rent increases should result in a net gain to the association, not merely a reduction in RDG. Accordingly, when considering claims for RDG, the Housing Corporation will assume that rents of assured tenancy lettings will be at the level of the association's average fair rents 'plus say 50 per cent of the excess of the actual rent over the average fair rent'. Perhaps this means 50 per cent above average fair rents?

The rent surplus fund

There was, under the previous arrangements, the requirement to keep a grant redemption fund (GRF). This is now abolished. Instead each association must keep a rent surplus fund (RSF) which will be different in important respects from the previous GRF.

The RSF arrangements will not apply to dwellings provided under the new HAG regime. Perhaps these are not expected to produce a surplus for some time yet. RSF rules apply, only to 'old HAG' schemes with their fair rents, where these are still charged, and the usually higher rents of houses re-let as assured tenancies. Gross rent income is calculated on the fair rents and, for re-lets, the higher of the actual rents is charged or the association's average fair rents. From this gross rent income will be deducted a four per cent allowance for voids and bad debts; loan charges; management and maintenance expenditure; service charges; miscellaneous items; rent losses which can arise when a new HAG dwelling is occupied by a tenant who retains security and fair rent rights.

From the net income thus calculated, the association can retain 70 per cent for transfer to a sinking fund to meet the cost of future major repairs. The rest is divided, 15 per cent each, between the Exchequer and the association for transfer to its reserves.

Under the previous grant redemption rules, 100 per cent of any surplus was liable to clawback by the Exchequer. So the new system will be welcome to the associations. The government, for its part, hopes that the new arrangements will prove an incentive to associations to increase their rents.

The outlook

Until now, the housing association movement has been seen by most people (including the DoE statistics section) as part of the public rented sector; and indeed it has been more dependent on public funding than council housing. Like council housing, it saw its purpose to provide for people who needed, or preferred, to rent, and its tenants have been as much in need of support from housing benefit as have council tenants.

It has been regarded as the voluntary movement at its best, non-profit making, motivated by social considerations, an admirable supplement to council housing, making a particularly valuable contribution to special categories such as the elderly and the single homeless, and widening the choice open to would-be tenants. It is now told that its future is as part of the 'independent rented sector' along with private and commercial landlords.

The movement has reacted to this with muted enthusiasm. The changes also mean an unprecedented involvement by the Housing Corporation in associations' affairs, even down to the scrutiny of their management performance. They are told that fair rents, which already 70 per cent of their tenants cannot pay without the help of housing benefit, are nevertheless much too low. They must in future give assured tenancies, and charge 'affordable' rents which are not defined except by a vague description as being within the reach of low income tenants. They are apprehensive that the new funding arrangements will be fraught with risk when they undertake new developments, save perhaps for the few large associations with sizeable reserves.

The new arrangements came into force in 1989, from 1 January for assured tenancies, and from 1 April for the new financial regime. Towards the end of the year there were reports that most housing associations had increased rents by 20 per cent, and some even by 30 per cent. Instances of abandoned schemes, prohibitive rents, and property sales were relatively few but they had begun to occur. Rent pooling, long established with council housing, was being actively considered by many associations in order to avoid the rapidly emerging 'split system' of fair rents for some and much higher rents for others. But this is a lot easier for some, such as Notting Hill Housing Trust which has a large stock (by housing association standards) of 8,000 dwellings and a small development programme, than it is for others. Some say that the new arrangements will oblige them to consider ability to pay, rather than housing need.

The general impression is one of uncertainty, a reluctance to jettison the thinking on which the movement has been based, and concern about the risks which the DoE and Housing Corporation seem to assume that the associations will readily accept on further developments. *An Inquiry into the Future of Housing Association Development in Central London* published in November 1989 is most timely in the light of these emerging anxieties.

It states that : ' *Housing associations are being expected to play a major role to fill the gap between the housing need of the middle and lower income groups and an open market in both owner-occupation and renting of housing. This expectation occurs at a time of a major change of central government policy direction from supply-side support (e.g. local authority housing) to the demand-side support (e.g. housing benefit)'*. (*"An Inquiry into the Future of Housing Association Development in Central London"* can be obtained from the Campaign for Homes in Central London (CHiCL), 5 Dryden Street, London WC2 9NW).

That, surely, goes to the heart of the matter. The previous system was designed to stimulate the provision of rented accommodation by providing a financial framework which ensured that the necessary resources would be available; that the arrangements would minimise the risks and uncertainties which development can involve; and they would bridge the gap between costs and fair rent levels. It was a highly successful example of the supply-side approach (to use the economists' current jargon), and it produced an extra 300,000 houses. The new system does none of these things.

The Private Rented Sector

At the outbreak of the first world war, renting was the normal tenure. It accounted for 90 per cent of the housing stock, with only ten per cent owner-occupied, a tiny amount of housing association dwellings, and virtually no council houses. By 1988, private renting had shrunk to about seven per cent, declining every year as privately rented dwellings were sold for owner-occupation or became unfit.

The General Household Survey (1986) found that 58 per cent of the privately rented stock had been built before 1919. It contained a far larger proportion of unsatisfactory accommodation than any other sector. 17.2 per cent was in serious disrepair, while 15.5 per cent was actually unfit for occupation.

This is a shocking state of affairs, and the reasons — largely financial — make a tangled and discreditable story.

In 1915, rents were frozen as a temporary war-time measure and tenants could not be evicted. But tenants were many and they all had votes, and landlords were few. What began as a temporary measure became a permanent feature of housing policy. Other countries had imposed rent control, but none behaved as ineptly as Britain which neither compensated landlords for lost income nor allowed rents to rise as incomes rose. Building for rent was already tailing off before 1914; other more attractive fields for investment had appeared. And rent control, in the rigid form it took, ensured that no sensible investor would put money into rented housing; and no landlord, when a property became vacant, would think of re-letting if they could sell. If the intention had been to destroy the private rented sector, no more effective strategy could have been devised.

This folly continued for over 40 years, with only quite inadequate rent increases allowed at long intervals, until in 1957 the Conservative government grasped the nettle. The Rent Act 1957 removed controls on dwellings above certain rateable values and on any property (whatever the rateable value) when a tenant left. This, it was claimed, would halt the decline of the private rented sector by giving landlords a fair return on their investment.

The government appeared to have completely overlooked that in conditions of serious scarcity, de-control would open the door to widespread exploitation, and a new word, 'Rachmanism', came into the English language as a result of the activities of one of the more unscrupulous operators in this field. Moreover, instead of stabilising, the sector began to decline faster than ever. As well as giving freedom to increase rents, de-control ended the tenant's security of tenure, so a landlord could get rid of a tenant and sell with vacant possession. This was a much more attractive proposition than re-letting, even at a high rent. Besides, might not some misguided future government reimpose control?

And this is exactly what happened.

Fair rents

Even before the Conservatives lost the 1964 election, they had become alarmed at the effects of the Rent Act 1957, and had set up the Milner Holland Committee to examine the Greater London housing problem; and they would have had to do something about it if they had been returned to office.

As soon as the new Labour government took office, it moved swiftly with a temporary holding measure restoring security of tenure and freezing existing rents. When the Milner Holland Committee report appeared in 1965, the government lost no time. The Minister concerned was Richard Crossman and his problem was that he could not simply return to the old controlled rents which were quite inadequate. Nor could he, in conditions of desperate scarcity, leave rents to market forces.

So he devised 'fair rents', a novel and entirely artificial concept. The Rent Act 1965 did not define a 'fair' rent, but where landlord and tenant could not agree on the rent level, a rent officer, appointed by the local authority, would decide what a fair rent should be.

In this exercise in the occult, the rent officer would ignore the personal circumstances of the tenant but have regard to the age, size, character, locality, and state of repair of the dwelling. They were required to set a rent which would be fair to both landlord and tenant as if supply and demand roughly balanced; in fact, a market rent in the absence of scarcity.

In the early days, most of the applications came from tenants, and the rent officers happily set about reducing large numbers of high rents which had resulted from the 1957 Act.

However, dissatisfied landlords or tenants could appeal to Rent Assessment Committees (RACs) appointed by the civil servants. Sir Sydney Littlewood, a well-known valuer, chaired the London Rent Assessment Committee (by far the most important), which set the tone for the other RACs. The London RAC increased many of the rents fixed by rent officers. Thereafter, it was mainly landlords, not tenants, who went to the rent officer asking them to set a 'fair' rent for their properties.

Not for the first time, the civil service had defeated the intentions of a Minister. Crossman was unhappy but went on claiming that his fair rent idea was basically sound. However, the disquiet was enough for the Labour government to set up another committee, the Francis Committee in 1969, to consider how the Rent Act 1965 was working. By the time it reported, two years later, a Conservative government was in power. The report concluded that although a lot of rent officers found themselves unable to quantify scarcity and therefore made no allowance for it, all was well — though allowing for the effect of scarcity had been the very basis of the Crossman formula. The report was accepted with alacrity.

The Conservative government went on to pass the Housing Finance Act 1972. This extended the fair rent concept to council housing (see chapter one) and it also made provision for a phased transfer of the remaining old controlled tenancies into the fair rent system called the 'regulated tenancy system'.

This phased transfer was halted temporarily by Labour when it returned to power in 1974, to give itself time to make a full review of the working of the Rent Acts, but it was all change once more, as a Conservative government took over in 1979.

Effects of the Housing Act 1980

By 1980, there were 400,000 houses still controlled under the old system. The Conservatives' 1980 Act converted them, at a stroke, to regulated tenancies for which fair rents would be set, whatever the condition of the properties. Landlords would also be allowed to apply for re-registration (for a higher rent) after two years, instead of three. It was the end of the original rent control system which had started in 1915 as a temporary measure.

Two new types of tenancy were also introduced. One was the protected shorthold tenancy, which allowed the landlord to let a vacant property at a fair rent for a fixed term of one to five years and regain possession at the end. It was expected that this would make shortholds an attractive proposition for landlords but it was not particularly successful. They still preferred to sell rather than re-let, since they were not happy with fair rents, even though these were likely to be three times as much as the previous controlled rents. After a couple of years, further legislation provided that, outside London, a landlord need not apply for a fair rent as a condition of letting on shorthold terms.

The other innovation was the assured tenancy. The fair rent system would not apply and rents would be freely negotiated between landlord and tenant. The landlord could let for any period, and at the end of the period the tenant would have a right to a new tenancy on terms to be agreed; or if not agreed, on terms to be settled by the County Court with any rent fixed by the Court set at market level.

At first, the assured tenancy applied only to new dwellings. In 1986, it was extended to existing dwellings if they had been improved or modernised by the landlord; but it was available only to landlords approved by the secretary of state.

It was claimed that these two new forms of tenancy would at last slow down, and perhaps even reverse, the decline of the private rented sector. But the downward trend continued, as table 5 shows:

Table 5

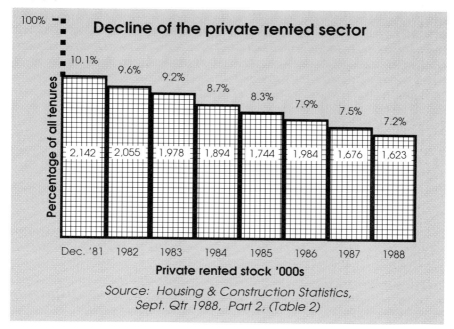

Source: Housing & Construction Statistics,
Sept. Qtr 1988, Part 2, (Table 2)

The Housing Act 1988

In 1987 the government issued a White Paper setting out its intentions for what was to become the Housing Act 1988. It covered all tenures.

On the private rented sector, the government proposed to de-regulate private lettings while protecting existing tenants. It planned to put new life into what it now calls the 'independent rented sector', housing owned by private landlords and housing associations. Public

59

sector housing would be dispersed to other landlords and the purchase and management of property by the private sector and housing associations would broaden the choice available to tenants.

While protecting the position of existing tenants, the government proposed to make progress towards market rents by building on the two concepts of assured and shorthold tenancies.

The changes made in pursuance of these objectives are set out in the Housing Act 1988, which came into effect on 15 January 1989.

For new lettings, the main change is that the regulated tenancy (subject to fair rents) no longer applies. Landlords can choose either:

▲ **an assured tenancy**, with rents freely negotiated but with security of tenure protected — at the end of a tenancy the tenant will be entitled to a further assured tenancy. A spouse will have an automatic right to succeed to the tenancy on the death of the assured tenant. There is no right to a second succession; and other relatives have no right at all to succeed.

▲ **an assured shorthold tenancy** for which the minimum period for letting has been reduced from one year to six months. There will not be a fair rent, though either party will have the right at any time to get the rent fixed at a 'market level which takes account of the limited security of tenure which the tenant has been offered'. Such a rent will be set by the Rent Assessment Committee.

Landlords offering assured tenancies no longer have to be approved by the Secretary of State, and the basic fitness standard has been abolished. Most of the remaining controls over new lettings by resident landlords (where the landlord lives in part of a dwelling and lets other parts) have been removed.

For existing tenancies the main changes are:

▲ **the fair rent system** still applies, but when a tenancy ends, the landlord can re-let on either an assured or assured shorthold basis.

▲ **the spouse will continue as the 'protected' tenant**, the new description for what was the 'regulated' tenant, when the tenant dies. Other relatives will have a right to succeed, but only if they have lived there for the last two years, and only as assured tenants. Second successions are only possible where the person was a member of both the original tenant's family and the first successor's family.

▲ **for existing shorthold tenants** there is no security of tenure beyond the brief period of the tenancy.

There are also provisions to protect tenants from harassment by landlords who seek to obtain possession or re-let at higher rents. And landlords will be entitled to charge 'key money', for the granting of assured or shorthold tenancy.

Housing benefit for private tenants

Housing benefit is paid by local councils to help private tenants on low incomes with their rents. Council tenants are also entitled to help. This system is described more fully in the next chapter.

Rents rose steeply as 'fair rents' replaced the old controlled rents and will rise even more steeply with assured and assured shorthold tenancies. They must do, since the government's declared aim is to raise rents high enough to reverse the decline of private renting.

Higher rents will obviously require higher housing benefit if serious hardship to tenants is to be avoided. The cost to the taxpayer will be substantial. There have been repeated assurances that housing benefit will continue to provide an adequate 'safety net', and the White Paper (para. 3.18) says that 'the housing benefit system will continue to provide help to those who need it'. But it also says that landlords should not be able to increase the rents of benefit recipients to unreasonable levels at the expense of the taxpayer.

The Housing Act 1988 requires rent officers to scrutinise the levels of rent which are being supported by housing benefit. When a rent is excessive, the local authority only gets subsidy on the appropriate market rent. The council, therefore, has to pay benefit based on the rent officer's concept of a market rent, not the landlord's. Not only will the rent officers decide what the market rent should be, they will also be required to consider whether the dwelling is too large for the tenant's 'reasonable' needs.

This is a sorry business. For low income tenants, assured rents are going to mean an assurance of more hardship, uncertainty and insecurity.

'Perks' for the private landlord

As long ago as 1985, the Greater London Council, just before its demise, did a survey which revealed that the majority of new lets in the London area were evading the Rents Act altogether by devices such as letting on licence, holiday lettings, or simply ignoring the law altogether and operating on a market rent basis. Nothing happened to them; and all that is happening now is that to a large extent their *modus operandi* is being legalised.

There is a further likely development. English and Welsh landlords will have read with interest how some of their colleagues in Scotland are taking seriously the government's concern about the need to make the private rented sector more attractive to landlords and investors.

They were mostly charging inclusive rents (i.e rent plus rates), and handing over the rates element to the local authority. Domestic rates ceased to be payable in Scotland from 1 April 1989 and have been replaced by the poll tax, so there is nothing to be handed over to the rating authority. Enterprising landlords have simply gone on charging as much as before, thus giving themselves a handsome rent increase, whilst the unfortunate occupiers will also be paying poll tax. So far, the government's only response to this scandalous business is an expression of pious hope that landlords will behave reasonably.

Will the government's policy work?

The aim of the government's policy is to stem, and if possible reverse, the decline in the private rented sector by allowing the charging of market rents for new lettings. Private landlords want, like other investors, not merely an adequate return on the amount originally invested but a return on the current value of their property.

Unfortunately, the government seems to be unaware that its policy is hopelessly flawed since, in seeking to meet the landlord's requirements, it depends on rent levels which most people who need to rent will not be able to pay. There is, dimly, a realisation that in present conditions the adequate 'safety net' which housing benefit should provide was never intended to cope with the situation which free markets will produce. Hence the new role for rent officers referred to above, which, if it means anything, will prevent market forces from operating freely.

There is also no apparent understanding that the tax privileges which subsidise home-ownership are not available to private landlords. It costs less to buy than to pay free market rents. Consider the elementary arithmetic.

Let us assume that a purchaser buys a house for £40,000. Mortgage interest is, at the time of writing, 14 per cent. The approximate annual outgoings with a 100 per cent mortgage for 25 years are shown in the table below.

A private landlord providing the same size and quality of house would have little chance of financing the operation so favourably, but assume 14 per cent for this comparison. The annual outgoings would be:

Table 6

Home-ownership versus renting

Homeowner's costs		Landlord's costs	
Mortgage repayments	5,800	Loan interest at 14 per cent	5,600
Less tax relief (£30,000 ceiling on mortgage so on £4,200 interest)	1,050	Maintenance, say	450
	4,750	Management, say	450
Repairs and maintenance, say	450		
(£100 per week)	£5,200	(£125 per week)	£6,500

£125 is unlikely to cover outgoings, let alone yield a profit. The rent, clearly, would have to be well over £125. Who is going to pay such a rent for a house that will never be theirs when £100 a week will buy it?

In London and the South-East the figures would be doubled, or more in some areas. There, the advantage in house purchase would be rather less, proportionately, because the £30,000 mortgage ceiling for tax relief would still apply on the much larger mortgage loan. But the advantage in buying would still be considerable; the landlord would need a rent which would be far beyond the reach of householders who need to rent.

Subsidies for some landlords?

Perhaps the government does, after all, recognise that subsidy for owner-occupation but not for private renting is one of the basic problems. In 1988 the then Chancellor, Nigel Lawson, extended the Business Expansion Scheme (BES) to rented housing. The scheme had been introduced to encourage the formation of small companies, but the rules were changed to allow the BES to apply to the provision of rented housing with a ceiling of investment of £5 million instead of the £500,000 which applies to other small businesses. There are limits on the prices of dwellings which may be bought under the scheme — £125,000 in London, £85,000 outside.

Tax relief is given at the marginal rate on investment in any year by an individual of up to £40,000. To increase the incentive in the first few months, the higher marginal rate, 60 per cent, applied if the investment was made by 26 October 1988. Since then it has been the current marginal rate, 40 per cent.

The practical effect is that with 40 per cent tax relief for example, the investor putting £40,000 into a scheme will get a reduction in their tax bill of £16,000; so the investment will cost only £24,000. To put it another way, for £24,000 invested there will be an added capital subsidy of £16,000.

As a further attraction, and to discourage early disinvestment, there is exemption from capital gains tax if the investor leaves the investment with the BES company for at least five years. The prospect of capital gains is, of course, a very important consideration.

The scheme will certainly bring additional private resources into the rented market, but the new landlords — often estate agents, solicitors and valuers — are unlikely to provide accommodation at 'affordable rents' for those with low incomes. They will offer assured tenancies where rents can be set at any level and some of them are quite frank about their intention to cater for the upwardly mobile who can afford market rents and can be expected to move on after a couple of years. The kind of rents being proposed so far — £350 a month for a one-bedroom flat, £450 for two-bedrooms — seem unlikely to be of any relevance to tenants who need help from the housing benefit system.

Nor does the scheme seem very likely to produce more housing. Most ventures so far appear to be concerned with acquiring existing properties. Nevertheless, the government does seem to have scored a 'first', breaking new ground by subsidising private landlords who provide rented accommodation for tenants who clearly could afford to be home-owners but not for tenants who must rent because home-ownership is not a possibility for them.

Housing Benefit

Today, most people who rent their homes rely on housing benefit to help them meet their housing costs. Housing benefit is a means-tested benefit aimed at those with the lowest incomes and which is rapidly withdrawn as income rises. Means-tested assistance has only been available to tenants in all tenures since 1972 and housing benefit itself has existed only since 1982. The introduction of housing benefit followed years of debate but, in the event, the scheme that was adopted had many shortcomings and it was implemented in so short a timescale that there was considerable administrative confusion. Less than a year after the full scheme started, a review was set up, and important changes were made to housing benefit as part of a wider reform of social security.

The Social Security Act 1986 led to the introduction of the reformed housing benefit system in April 1988. Further changes took effect from April 1990 (1989 in Scotland), when rate rebates were replaced by community charge benefit (which is not strictly part of housing benefit, since the poll tax is not a tax on property).

Background

Housing is expensive and the origins of housing benefit lie in debates in the early part of this century about how best to help low income households to afford decent accommodation. The introduction of housing subsidies in 1919 meant that the rents of council houses were generally lower than they would otherwise have been but, at first, there was no attempt to ensure that subsidies helped the least well off. Indeed, in the 1920s, the costs of building new houses were so high that even subsidised rents were generally beyond the reach of the poor. Council housing thus began as subsidised housing for the rather better off skilled workers.

However, in 1930 the Labour Government passed a Housing Act requiring councils to launch slum clearance programmes. Rehousing families from the slums inevitably meant that councils became landlords to growing numbers of poorer people. The government therefore gave way to demands to provide rent rebates for those who could least afford the rent of a new council house.

Councils could grant rent rebates on whatever terms they chose; there was no compulsion to provide rebates nor any clear guidance on the form that rebate schemes might take. And there was no central government subsidy to pay for rebates; if an authority chose to grant rent rebates to certain tenants then it did so either by redistributing existing general Exchequer subsidy or by increasing the amount contributed from the rates in support of housing. Central government was not, at that time, strongly committed to means-tested rent assistance. The 1930 Act set a pattern which endured for forty years, until the introduction of a mandatory rent rebate scheme, with its own specific subsidy in 1972.

During the 1930s, both councils and their tenants were opposed to rent rebate schemes and for a while, after the second world war, interest in providing rebates declined still further. It was in the mid-1950s that a Conservative government revived debate about the best way to provide help with housing costs. The Conservative Party has always regarded the universal provision of public services, like health care and education, as wasteful. It emphasised the targeting of public resources on those in greatest need and in the mid-1950s it urged councils to extend the availability of rent rebate schemes while raising rents generally. There was an important policy shift away from general subsidy and towards means-tested benefits.

However, if help with housing costs was to be means-tested, should the local authorities be responsible for providing such help? In the 1950s and 1960s, there was a protracted disagreement between local authorities and the National Assistance Board (replaced by the Supplementary Benefits Commission in 1966). The local authority view was that rebates were a social security benefit and should be provided by the appropriate authority. The NAB argued that councils had a responsibility to distribute housing subsidies to those in need of such help. This long-running dispute illustrates the ambiguity of rent rebates, occupying as they do the ground where housing and social security meet. It also highlights the development of two quite separate, but overlapping systems, of providing help with housing costs.

The need to resolve this problem was intensified after 1972. Local authorities had to provide rent rebates for their own tenants and give rent allowances for private tenants. Before this, there had been no help for private tenants who were working or who, for other reasons, did not qualify for supplementary benefit. Many more tenants now became eligible for benefit.

The parallel existence of the local authority and social security systems also gave rise to what became known as the 'better off' problem. Councils gave rent rebates and rent allowances on a means test which took into account *gross* income while supplementary benefit operated on a measure of *net* income. Also, the rebate/allowance scheme was more generous than supplementary benefit to people on rather higher incomes. This was a recipe for confusion. Although many people qualified for both benefits, they could only receive one and they had to choose whether to claim a rebate/allowance or supplementary benefit but it was often difficult to tell which would make them better off. It was even difficult for skilled housing advisers to decide which benefit people should claim.

The 'better off problem' resulted in hundreds of thousands of people receiving the 'wrong' benefit, and this became one of the main reasons for reform which could produce a unified housing benefit. In the late 1970s, the Supplementary Benefits Commission argued for a unified benefit to be administered by the local housing authorities. As well as producing a simpler and fairer system, the SBC wanted it to provide help for low income home-owners who were generally ignored by the existing systems. Home-owners could claim rate rebates, and the few who were entitled to supplementary benefit could be helped with mortgage interest, but most low income home-owners were very unfairly treated by the system of mortgage interest tax relief which was so generous to higher earners.

When the Conservative government produced its proposals (*Assistance with Housing Costs*, 1981) they were largely confined to administrative reform in all sectors. The opportunity for fundamental reform of housing finance was spurned in favour of a limited reorganisation of responsibilities for the administration of housing benefits plus a certain amount of redistribution towards the poorest at the expense of the slightly better off.

The housing benefit scheme was introduced in two stages, in November 1982 and April 1983, following the Social Security and Housing Benefits Act 1982. *The Times* described it as '*the biggest administrative fiasco in the history of the welfare state.*' (20 January 1984). This was the result of numerous factors but mostly the complexity of the new system and the speed with which it was introduced. Councils were simply not given enough time, nor enough help, to allow them to implement the system successfully. The government then made a series of cuts in the benefit levels which made it even more difficult for councils and claimants alike.

The new scheme retained the two separate means tests that were inherited from the old system. After 1982 there were two categories of housing benefit claimant, known as 'standard' and 'certificated' cases. Standard housing benefit was effectively the old rent rebate (or allowance) and rates rebate, while certificated housing benefit was like the housing part of supplementary benefit. These two separate forms of housing benefit, based on different means tests, meant that people with similar incomes could be treated quite differently depending on whether they were entitled to supplementary benefit or not.

The current housing benefit scheme

A review of the 1982 scheme was completed in 1985 and proposals were incorporated into the Social Security Act 1986. This Act also reformed other parts of the social security system including the replacement of supplementary benefit by income support and the introduction of the social fund; family credit replaced family income supplement.

The new housing benefit scheme was designed to be simpler to administer and understand; to treat people in similar circumstances in the same way whether or not they were working: to direct help to

Housing Benefit '86

TO ILLUSTRATE HOW THE SCHEME WORKS, THIS IS A PLAN OF HAMPTON COURT MAZE....

where it was most needed; to improve accountancy; and to encourage efficient administration.

The new scheme is better than the pre-1988 system as there is no longer a distinction between standard and certificated cases. All claimants are now assessed on the basis of the income support means test. Where a claimant's income is equivalent to, or less than, what is known as the 'applicable amount', then housing benefit provides 100 per cent of eligible housing costs (i.e. in most cases HB covers the full rent).

As income rises above the applicable amount, the level of benefit is reduced. In the jargon of social security, benefit is said to 'taper', and in the case of housing benefit it tapers at a rate of 65p for every £1 of extra income. So, if a person was entitled to housing benefit of £10 per week, they would lose all entitlement when their income reached an extra £16 a week. (16 x 0.65 = £10.40).

For community charge, or poll tax, benefit (CCB), the maximum level of help is 80 per cent and the rate of taper is 15 per cent. So, a person claiming both HB and CCB would find that their benefit was reduced by 80p for every extra £1 of income. To understand how the scheme works it is useful to look at who can claim HB, how the scheme is administered, how claims are calculated and how benefit is paid.

The housing benefit scheme applies to both public and private sector tenants. This covers a wide range of landlords, including councils, housing associations, new towns, commercial landlords, co-ops and hostels. Home-owners who previously got HB for rates can now only claim the separate community charge benefit.

There are two routes to claiming housing benefit. People claiming income support normally claim HB (and CCB) at the same time from the Department of Social Security (DSS). But housing benefit is not administered by the DSS so forms have to be passed on to the local authorities which are the responsible agencies. The second route to claiming is, therefore, to make a direct approach to the local authority. People not claiming income support usually do this.

Councils must take several things into account when assessing a claim. Claimants on income support are easiest to assess because details such as income and capital assets will have been verified by the DSS when they assess the income support claim, before the papers are passed to the local council. However, the council still has to investigate the person's rent and poll tax, and details of any non-dependent adults living in the same house. People on income support get maximum benefit which covers eligible rent, minus any deduction for non-dependents, and 80 per cent of poll tax. For instance, a single person with a rent of £30 per week and a poll tax liability of £7 per week will be able to claim £30 rent (100% housing benefit) and £5.60 community charge benefit (80% rebate). This claimant has to find £1.40 per week towards the poll tax. People not on income support might have to pay significant amounts towards both rent and poll tax, depending on their circumstances. To calculate their entitlement, the council has to determine income; capital; the 'applicable amount'; eligible costs; details of any non-dependents.

Income is calculated on weekly income from all sources such as wages, benefits, pensions, and assumed (not actual) interest on savings above £3000. Some forms of income are disregarded. The term capital applies to savings, property, shares and any lump sum payments from redundancy or retirement. Anyone with more than £16,000 of capital cannot get either HB or CCB but some capital is disregarded, most notably the claimant's home.

The 'applicable amount' is the official measure of the amount that people in different circumstances need in order to meet basic living requirements. The applicable amount for any particular claimant is a combination of the relevant personal allowance plus any relevant premiums. In 1990-91, the personal allowance for a single person over the age of 25 is £36.70, and for a couple where at least one partner is over 18, £57.60. There are different dependents' allowances for each child in a family. The premiums are extra amounts in recognition of higher costs for certain claimants and households. So, there are premiums for lone parents, disabled children, disabled adults, and pensioners.

Eligible costs cover rent and poll tax. Since the deregulation of private sector rents at the start of 1989, rent officers have stopped fixing fair rents for new lettings and have the job of determining market rents for HB purposes (see also chapter three). In cases where the claimant's accommodation is too large, or where the rent is unreasonably high compared with rents for suitable alternative accommodation, the council is not obliged to pay HB on the full rent. The eligible rent then would be set by the rent officer rather than the market.

The final item to be considered is any non-dependents living in the claimant's household. Certain categories of non-dependents are assumed to be making a contribution to the rent and reductions are made in the claimant's HB entitlement, depending on the circumstances of the non-dependent.

It is now possible to present another example, this time referring to a couple with two children aged seven and eleven, one of whom is disabled. The man is assumed to be working full-time, earning £160 per week. They have savings of under £3,000, and so there is no notional income from interest. Rent is £30 per week and poll tax is £7 per week per adult.

Table 7

Housing benefit — a specimen calculation

Personal allowances	£	Income for benefit purposes	£
Couple	57.60	Gross earnings per week	160.00
Child under 11	12.35	Less tax and N I	24.32
Child 11 - 15	18.25	Net earnings per week	135.68
	88.20	Less income disregard	10.00
Plus premiums			125.68
Family	7.35	Plus child benefit	14.50
Disabled child	15.40		
Total applicable amount	110.95	Total net income	140.18

An income of £140.18 less applicable amount of £110.95 leaves £29.23. This family thus has income which is £29.23 above their applicable amount. Their housing benefit and community charge benefit are therefore reduced by the relevant tapers applied to this excess income. So, for housing benefit, their eligible rent (100 per cent of their rent) of £30 is reduced by the rent taper applied to their excess income (65 per cent of £29.23 = £19). This gives them housing benefit of £11.

For community charge benefit, their eligible poll tax is 80 per cent of their total weekly poll tax bill of £14 which is £11.20. This is reduced by the community charge benefit taper applied to their excess income (15 per cent of £29.23 = £4.38). This gives them a community charge benefit of £6.82.

Their total benefit is therefore £17.82, on outgoings for rent and poll tax of £44, leaving them to find £26.18 themselves.

This is just one example, and different circumstances will give different results. For a more detailed explanation, it is best to read one of the specialist books such as the Guide to Housing Benefit and Community Charge Benefit 1990-91 by Martin Ward and John Zebedee (Institute of Housing/SHAC, £6.95).

Paying for housing benefit

Until 1972, local authorities were not given any specific financial support for paying rebates to poorer tenants and had to use general housing subsidy to fund rebates. From 1972 onwards there was a specific rent rebate subsidy but it was not until the introduction of HB in 1982 that the government moved rent rebate subsidy into the social security budget within the national public expenditure accounts. This made good sense because it left the DoE responsible for housing subsidy and the DHSS (later the DSS) took on responsibility for what was properly recognised as a social security benefit. It would have been logical to take the next step and to transfer *administrative* responsibility for HB to the DSS as well.

However, in the Local Government and Housing Act 1989, the government took several paces backwards by merging rent rebate subsidy with housing subsidy in the new housing revenue account subsidy. Rent rebate subsidy was calculated by looking at the entitlements of all the individual council tenants claiming HB and this continues to be the case. However, since April 1990, HRA subsidy is paid only to balance the HRA, and if gross rents (rents actually paid by tenants, plus rebates) exceed notional expenditure, then the full cost of rebates will not be paid by the Exchequer. In extreme cases, it is possible that rebated rents will cover total expenditure and the Exchequer will pay out nothing at all!

Critics of the government's position have argued that the better off tenants will thus find themselves paying the rebates of their poorer neighbours. It has also been argued that this move reflects Treasury determination to get its hands on any HRA surpluses rather than allowing councils to use them to improve local services.

There is another flaw in the current system as it applies to the private sector. The government's aim was to establish a deregulated private rented market but there is a conflict between a free market and a benefit system which provides 100 per cent assistance to the poorest tenants. If some tenants are guaranteed all their housing costs, then there is no market-based restraint on rents which is why the government has had to divert the rent officer service into the task of fixing maximum rents for benefit purposes.

The obvious way forward in this situation would be to reimpose a system based on regulated rents in the private sector but that, of course, would require a change of government.

5 Owner Occupation

By 1990, owner-occupation accounted for 15.1 million dwellings, just over 66 per cent of the housing stock, by far the fastest growing and most popular sector. This is not surprising, for not only does it offer the householder more freedom and choice than any other tenure, it has also long been the most profitable investment that ordinary people ever make.

The extent of the expansion has been spectacular:

Table 8

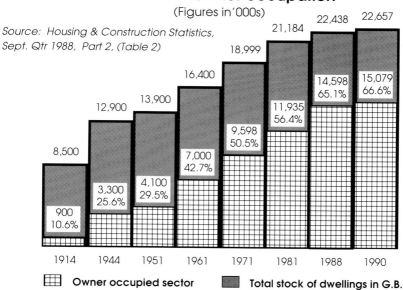

Increase in owner occupation
(Figures in'000s)

Source: Housing & Construction Statistics, Sept. Qtr 1988, Part 2, (Table 2)

1914	1944	1951	1961	1971	1981	1988	1990

Total stock of dwellings: 8,500 / 12,900 / 13,900 / 16,400 / 18,999 / 21,184 / 22,438 / 22,657

Owner occupied: 900 (10.6%) / 3,300 (25.6%) / 4,100 (29.5%) / 7,000 (42.7%) / 9,598 (50.5%) / 11,935 (56.4%) / 14,598 (65.1%) / 15,079 (66.6%)

⊞ Owner occupied sector   ▨ Total stock of dwellings in G.B.

The provision of housing requires massive finance. Virtually all houses are bought with borrowed money, and until recent years, nearly all of this came from building societies. Local authorities, insurance companies and banks made a relatively small contribution. However, there have been enormous changes since the early 1980s with the banks especially making a dramatic increase in their share of the market.

Although the building societies' share of the business has declined recently to between 50 and 60 per cent, it is still by far the largest; and it has been the societies which developed the procedures which all the market follow. We start by looking at the way they operate.

Growth of the building societies

Building societies started in a small way in the 19th century with small groups of working people joining together, each member paying a weekly subscription. When there was enough money to buy or build a house, one of the members would take it over, and so on until all had been housed. Each would continue to contribute until all had been dealt with and the group would then disband. These early societies were called 'terminating' societies, and out of their success developed the 'permanent' societies, raising funds by offering a savings bank facility. But progress was still very slow until after the end of the first world war when their expansion really started. Yet this was

Table 9

	Building societies' progress	
	Source: Housing Finance July 1989 (Council of Mortgage Lenders)	
	Advances during year £m	Total assets at year end £m
1900	9	60
1920	25	87
1940	21	756
1960	560	3,166
1980	9,614	53,793
1988	49,376	188,844

as nothing to what followed the second world war or even the more explosive growth of the last twenty years *(see Table 9)*.

In earlier years there were some colourful characters in the industry — not a bit like it is today — and there were some spectacular (and sometimes hilarious) episodes involving fraud. But the dramatic success of the last thirty years has been solidly built on a first rate service to savers and a reputation for reliability. The privileged tax position (see later) has helped too.

The way lenders work

At first sight, the whole basis on which building societies have operated, accepting money which is mostly repayable on demand or at very short notice, and lending it for long periods, is the very opposite of what is normally regarded as sound practice. It is borrowing short to lend long. But there is a safeguard which transforms the situation. Each loan is secured by a mortgage. It gives a 'legal charge'to the lender on the property by which, if the borrower fails to comply with the terms of the mortgage, the lender can take over the property (called foreclosing), sell it, and clear the debt from the proceeds of the sale. The mortgage also contains a 'variable interest clause', and it is this which allows the lenders to make loans for 25 years or even more, although the greatest part of their funds come from investors who are entitled to repayment immediately, or at very short notice.

When interest rates rise, the lending institution can avoid withdrawals by investors by promptly increasing its own interest rates to investors. It can do this quite safely because it can at the same time give notice to all its borrowers, under the variable interest clause in their mortgages, that the interest they pay will also go up.

In practice, the conditions which result in changes in interest rates for investors will affect all lending institutions, and the building societies until 1983 published recommended rates of interest to give a measure of stability in a vast financial market which affects millions of people. The members of the Building Societies Association followed the recommendations fairly closely.

Until recently, repayment of loans by the borrowers was usually by a repayment mortgage. This operated on the annuity method, an equalised payment of interest and principal combined over the whole life of the loan. Interest is on the amount outstanding on the loan. In the first year it will be on the whole amount of the loan plus a very small amount towards repayment of the principal. At first the interest element takes up by far the largest share of the mortgage repayments, but as the years go by and the interest element decreases while the principal element increases, the latter becomes the dominating share of the repayment. The whole calculation ensures that by the end of the period, the loan will have been paid off.

There is another method, which is increasingly popular, called the endowment mortgage. This has a variable interest clause and gives security to the lender as with the repayment mortgage. But instead of repaying the principal a little at a time, the borrower takes out an assurance policy which, besides giving life assurance cover during the loan period, will at the end of the term yield a sum which will pay off the loan. So the method means paying interest on the whole amount of the loan throughout the loan period, and an annual premium on the assurance policy.

Some building societies charge interest at slightly higher rates than for repayment mortgages because, presumably, foregoing regular payments of principal means tying up substantial sums for long periods.

As would be expected, the endowment method costs more than the annuity method, but the borrowers (and dependents) have the valuable safeguard of life assurance cover, and hopefully, surplus cash at the end of the period.

Tax relief on the mortgage interest will be much greater than with a repayment mortgage because it will not decrease year by year, since the interest will not decrease as it does with the annuity method. By 1981, about a quarter of borrowers were choosing the endowment mortgage; by 1989 it was about 80 per cent.

One of the largest building societies gives the following examples of the relative costs of repayment mortgages and low-cost endowment mortgages (*see table 10*)

The figures show monthly repayments net of tax on the interest at standard rate. There is a tax relief ceiling of the interest chargeable on a £30,000 mortgage; so the £30,000 mortgages in the examples are receiving tax relief on *all* the interest; the £60,000 examples have relief on only *half* the interest. The loan period is 25 years in each case. A fractionally lower interest rate is quoted for the larger loans. Some lenders have this policy, presumably because administration costs are no higher on a large amount than on a small amount.

It should be noted that the endowment mortgage examples assume a couple age 30. The older the borrower, the higher will be the premium.

Table 10

Typical mortgage costs

	Repayment Mortgage		Low Cost Endowment	
Mortgage				
Amount of Loan	£30,000	£60,000	£30,000	£60,000
Current interest rate	15.4%	14.75%	15.4%	14.75%
Monthly payments				
Principal and				
net interest	318.65	688.38	—	—
net interest	—	—	288.75	645.31
Endowment Premium	—	—	40.90	80.80
Total Monthly Payments	318.65	688.38	329.65	726.11

The lending on endowment mortgages is done by the building society, bank or other lender, with the life assurance cover provided by an insurance company. There have been criticisms that the rapid expansion of the method is not wholly unconnected with the fact that lenders, estate agents and solicitors earn a substantial commission from the insurance company on policies sold.

One feature peculiar to building societies until 1985 was that the interest they paid to their investors was 'tax paid'. This meant that the Inland Revenue treated it as if tax at standard rate had been deducted from it. Recipients were therefore not liable for any tax on it unless they were liable for tax above the standard rate. If they were, they would be charged for the difference between standard rate and whatever was their top rate. While the standard rate of tax is 25 per cent, then, 7.5 per cent tax paid is worth 10 per cent gross.

Any other organisation that deducted tax from interest or dividends paid out had to hand over precisely whatever tax had been deducted. Building societies alone did not; they handed over at a lower rate, called the composite rate, and so made a useful surplus on the operation.

This odd arrangement came about long ago, before 1894, in the days when income tax was 4p in the pound. It suddenly occurred to the Inland Revenue that no tax was being paid on interest received by building society investors. It did not even know who these people were. So it asked how much was being paid, and to whom, so that it could tax it. The building societies were deeply shocked, refused to give this confidential information and went on refusing for years.

However, as everyone knows, the tax gatherers are ruthless people and they came along in 1894 with a proposal to tax the profits of building societies. This so alarmed the societies that they offered to account for tax on interest paid out at half rate. This was a rough and ready method of recognising that some investors would be taxable, some not. The Inland Revenue was happy. It would get its money, or most of it, and save itself a lot of clerical work.

The building societies were also happy. They have been getting a concealed subsidy by not having to hand over tax at the full standard rate. But the banks were not happy, and argued, reasonably, that the composite rate gave the societies an unfair advantage (as it clearly did). In the 1940s, when the standard rate was 50 per cent, the composite rate was 30 per cent, and this was worth as much as two per cent on building society borrowing. But times change. For 1988-89, with the standard rate at 25 per cent, the composite rate was 23.25 per cent. The concealed subsidy is nothing like it was but is still a useful 0.3 or 0.4 per cent reduction in the cost of borrowing.

The fair thing to do would have been to abolish the composite rate, require building societies to hand over tax at standard rate, and allow non-taxable investors to claim repayment. But this would have made more work for the Inland Revenue, so instead, the government in April 1985 actually extended the system to banks, local authorities, and some other financial institutions.

The borrowers

Most would-be home-owners, having found a suitable house, approach a lender for a loan. Lenders used to be prepared to lend 75 per cent, perhaps 80 per cent, of the value of the property. Borrowers would have to find the rest themselves as well as other costs like solicitors' and valuers' fees.

The lender wants to ensure that the borrower will be able to meet the cost of repayments, and for many years a common measure was that a loan could be up to 2.25 — 2.5 times the borrower's annual income. If there were two incomes involved, usually the second income, or part of it, could be taken into account. Earnings of say

£8,000 a year would have been good for a loan of £18,000 to £20,000, if the value of the property justified it.

That was the position until about 1984 but the house price explosion has made for great changes. It has meant vastly increased demand in terms of finance, not only from the first-time buyers but also from owners who see an advantage in 'trading up' to larger or better quality dwellings. Incomes have been rising too. And building societies and other lenders, observing the unprecedented rise in house prices, have felt secure in the knowledge that the value of their security — the dwelling — was rising rapidly, and they now felt safe in lending three times the annual income. And this was three times a larger income than it would have been two or three years earlier. The change in the general picture has been considerable:

Former owner-occupiers usually have higher incomes than first-

Table 11

Building society loan advances

Source: Housing Finance July 1989 (Council of Mortgage Lenders)

	Number of advances	Average income of buyer	Average dwelling price	Average advance	Advance as % of dwelling	Advance times income
	000s	£	£	£	%	

First time buyers

1977	355	4,800	10,857	8,515	78.4	1.8
1986	619	11,669	27,444	23,640	86.1	2.0
1987	505	12,444	30,097	25,485	84.7	2.0
1988	580	13,990	35,807	30,374	84.8	2.2

Former owner-occupiers

1977	382	5,558	16,246	9,101	56.0	1.6
1986	612	4,165	45,200	27,146	60.2	1.9
1987	542	15,004	49,987	29,487	59.0	2.0
1988	650	17,108	61,540	36,013	58.5	2.1

time buyers. They are now able to put down £25,000 on average towards the cost of a house, from the proceeds of the sale of the former house, as compared with about £5,000 in the case of first time buyers. Existing owner-occupiers do not mind the house price explosion at all.

Subsidies for owner-occupiers

An astonishing number of people still refuse to believe that home-ownership gets any help from the public purse, while complaining about 'subsidised council tenants'. Yet the government does not deny that the tax system provides massive subsidy; it confines itself to asserting its determination to preserve present arrangements without change of any sort. Opposition parties stress their awareness of the importance of home-ownership and the need to make such help as is given, more effective.

PROBLEM WITH YOU COUNCIL TENANTS IS YOU'RE A FLIPPIN' BURDEN ON THE TAXPAYER!!

Schedule A tax

The ownership of property always used to be taxed on its rental value. The tax was called Schedule A tax, as distinct from Schedule D which is levied on profits, or Schedule E on earnings.

Owner-occupiers do not pay rent. Of two people in identical houses, worth a rent of say £2,000 a year, one owning and one renting, the owner will have £2,000 a year more to spend than the one who is a tenant. It has been argued that the owner has sacrificed income by putting money into buying a house instead of investing it in some other way. That is perfectly true. But if the money had been invested so that it produced £2,000 annual income there would have been tax to pay on that income; whereas no tax is payable on the no less real increase in disposable income which results from owning instead of renting.

There was a problem with Schedule A. The Inland Revenue took the easy way out by using rating values as the measure of letting value and this would have been a sensible avoidance of unnecessary valuation work if rating values had been kept up to date. But they never were. All governments shirk the unpopularity of revaluation. In the post-war years annual rental values for rating had become a mere fraction of real rental values, so Schedule A tax produced much less revenue than it should have done.

In 1955, a Royal Commission on the Taxation of Profits and Income considered the problem and recommended that taxation of the benefit of ownership (on what it called the 'imputed rental') was right, and should continue as an essential element of a fair taxation system.

Nevertheless, in 1963, when Parliament considered the issue, it decided that it was not right to tax a person on a rent they did not collect and, ignoring all the reasoning in the Commission report, it abolished Schedule A income tax. And anyway, the tax was not producing much revenue (and no wonder).

Since then, the owner has enjoyed a tax-free increase in net disposable income as compared with what happens to a tenant. They are being given favourable treatment, as compared with other householders who have to pay rent, by being relieved of tax which should be paid if there is to be tax neutrality between one taxpayer and another; by being subsidised. For that tax foregone means that taxpayers generally have to pay more to make good what is lost.

Tax relief on mortgage interest

A householder, while the legal owner, might not own outright, if the property is still on mortgage. There is ownership in a legal sense, but in practical terms the householder is only in the process of *becoming* the owner, not yet enjoying the full benefits of ownership. It would clearly not be equitable to tax mortgagors as if they did own outright. They were saving themselves a rent but they had to meet repayments on a mortgage.

This had not been a problem. In accordance with normal taxation practice, though mortgagors were taxable under Schedule A as owners, they were entitled to a reduction of the assessment in respect of the interest being paid on the mortgage loan. In the parlance of the tax people, they were entitled to set off the expense incurred in *acquiring* an asset against any tax levied on income arising from *ownership* of that asset.

So when Parliament abolished Schedule A tax, there remained no logical reason for giving tax relief on mortgage interest. But Parliament is nothing if not resilient and this little local difficulty scarcely gave it pause. There was still every justification for continuing the relief, it was said, because the interest was being paid out of income which had already been taxed. That this principle could also then logically apply to rents, or a holiday on the Costa Brava, which are also paid out of income which has already been taxed, did not occur to them.

Some members advanced a second argument. Owner-occupation is a good thing in itself and should be encouraged. Tax relief on mortgage interest may be a subsidy, but if it is, it is justified because home-ownership deserves subsidising. All parties agreed. Schedule A tax was abolished. Tax relief on mortgage interest remained.

There is nothing wrong in principle with assisting home-ownership. What has been wrong, and dishonest, is the constant stressing of the heavy cost of subsidies to council tenants as if these increased the burden on the taxpayer whilst tax concessions to owner-occupiers did not. The situation has become worse year after year, as housing subsidies for rented houses are reduced whilst the cost of tax relief for house purchase increases at an ever more alarming rate. The cost was reported by ministers to be the gigantic sum of £8,000 million in 1990/91 for relief on mortgage interest alone.

M I R A S

Before 1983, mortgagors got tax relief on mortgage interest by a reduction in their tax bill up to a permitted maximum (in recent years of interest on a £30,000 loan). Someone liable only for tax at the standard rate got relief at the standard rate. Someone who paid tax at a higher rate got relief at the top rate.

In April 1983 the system was changed by the introduction of MIRAS (Mortgage interest relief at source).

Mortgagors paid interest reduced by tax at the standard rate, and the building societies were reimbursed by the Exchequer for lost income.

But the MIRAS system gives tax relief at the standard rate to those mortgagors in a higher tax bracket, so they get extra help by a reduction in their tax bill as well as in their mortgage. The anomaly of most help for those with the highest incomes, who need it least, has been carefully preserved.

Other tax privileges for owner-occupiers

The sale of any asset normally results in liability to capital gains tax on any profits from the sale. Home-ownership, where the home is the principal dwelling of the seller, is exempt. The cost of this exemption was estimated by the Treasury to be worth £2,200 million in 1985-86. By 1988-89, after three years of steep increases in house prices, the estimate was £10,000 million, dwarfing even the huge cost of tax relief on mortgage interest, and making the cost of subsidies on council houses a mere bagatelle.

Owning a home as an investment

Ownership has so far been the perfect hedge against inflation, in that the housebuyer's costs are mainly mortgage repayments and these are fixed, not on the current value of the dwelling, but on the amount borrowed when the house was bought. It is this characteristic of home-ownership — annual costs based on the historic cost — that is its most important and valuable feature.

Consider someone who bought the average new house in 1975, the price being £12,000, interest then 11 per cent, loan period 25 years. That house today will fetch £50,000.

Mortgage repayments will have fluctuated as interest rates have changed, down to 8.5 per cent at one stage, as high as 15 per cent on other occasions. Nevertheless, it has been putting on an average of £2,700 per year in value, over twice as much as the annual mortgage repayments ever since it was bought. And in a few years the mortgage repayments will end, leaving the owner with a debt-free, rent-free, high-value asset.

No wonder home ownership is highly regarded.

Other considerations

But is there another side to the coin? House prices now (late 1990) have ceased to rise, interest rates are at a record high, further increases are possible, many recent purchasers are suffering financial hardship, housebuilding is in the doldrums, and home-owners who need to move elsewhere are having serious problems as transactions grind to a halt.

Young people who need a home cannot afford to buy at present prices, and cannot find a house to rent because there is such a shortage of rented accommodation because council housebuilding has virtually ceased, and housing association building is much reduced.

There is cause for concern there as there should be about the sheer magnitude of housing credit — a staggering £221 billion at the end of 1988, of which the building societies share £155 billion. Outstanding housing debt has increased by 142 per cent in five years (from £91.6 billion to £221.7 billion), yet the number of owner-occupiers is up by only 14 per cent (12.9 million in 1983, 14.7 million in 1988). That's the effect of the house price spiral for you. The money has mainly been going to re-finance existing dwellings when they change hands; only one advance in ten in 1988 was a newly-built house. It is not clear what effect on these figures will result from the dramatic slowdown in the housing market which has now appeared.

6 Overview

In considering the financial arrangements for housing, it is necessary first to remember its special characteristics.

Housing — special features

Housing is what economists call a durable commodity, unlike for example food and drink, or semi-durable commodities like cars or washing machines. Its length of life — for practical purposes only land has a longer life — makes it almost unique. The effect of inflation (a permanent condition, apparently) is particularly important for, instead of houses losing value as they grow older, their value in money terms actually grows. And over the last 20 years the growth has been spectacular.

There are other factors besides inflation which affect house prices. There is the availability or scarcity of mortgage funds from building societies and banks, or the sudden variations of mortgage interest rates. And there is the desperate scarcity of rented property in many areas which increases the pressure on house prices by obliging numbers of people who, cannot really afford it, to buy.

The steady pressure of demand for housing, whether for renting or buying, should in theory produce increased supply. Thus will the market, operating freely, solve the problem. There are people who really believe this despite the evidence of their own eyes. Unfortunately for them, housing demonstrates another unhelpful characteristic — supply is 'inelastic', i.e. it cannot be increased rapidly. Whatever the demand, the size of the housing stock grows by not more than two per cent a year. At present, thanks to the unprecedented restrictions imposed by government on councils and some reduction in housing association provision, the annual increase is rather less than one per cent.

Housing cannot safely be left to market forces. Before the first world war, before anyone even thought of rent control, market forces operated. Yet the country faced shortages, slums, over-crowding, disrepair, and lack of basic amenities. Seventy years of effort since 1919 have raised standards enormously for most people but have never fully overcome the problems. In 1990 council housing waiting lists are as long as ever; there is a record and growing number of families accepted by councils as homeless; and in many cities large and growing numbers of young single people, not eligible under law for help as homeless persons and affected by recent drastic reductions in social security provision, are reduced to sleeping rough. It is a shocking indictment of government housing policies in the last ten years.

Ever since the first world war, it has been accepted that decent

housing standards are an essential condition of a just and healthy society, and indeed, are as necessary a feature of an efficient advanced industrial society such as ours as effective health, education and welfare services. There was, for much of the time, national consensus about this, though different parties attached different emphasis at times to various aspects of housing policies.

But alas for good intentions, housing is such a significant element in terms of the resources it requires that governments have never been able to resist using housing policies as tools in their attempts at overall management of the nation's economy.

Visible and invisible subsidies

In Britain, the cost of subsidies to council housing has been a constant topic for government ministers. The cost of subsidising home-ownership, on the other hand, is seldom mentioned; when it is, it is only to say that home-owners have entered into commitments in the expectation that the system will continue unchanged, and they can rest content that this will be so. A Labour government Green Paper, 'Housing Policy: a consultation document' in 1977 gave the same assurance.

The Treasury says tax relief is not a subsidy. A subsidy is an actual payment, whereas this tax is foregone. This is very reassuring until it is realised that the effect is precisely the same. The payment of a subsidy increases the disposable income of the fortunate recipient; and so does tax relief.

An American writer, W C Baer, referred in 1975 to 'the comparison between the highly visible, contentious, grudgingly given, inflexible and cumbersome housing subsidies to renters, and the unstigmatised, back-door, low profile, popular and highly effective tax benefits to some buyers'.

He was talking about America. It's a small world.

How it looks to economists

Academic economists point to two features of housing — the investment aspect, which is involved in the provision of a dwelling; and the consumption aspect, which is the use and benefit of the accommodation.

With private rented housing, (as with council housing), the landlord bears the cost of provision. This investment results in ownership of an asset which will produce an income, the rent, paid by the tenant. The landlord has the ownership, the tenant has the use.

In considering what the rent should be, most economists favour market rents. The rental value of a dwelling is what people are prepared to pay for the use of it, irrespective of what it cost the owner to acquire it. Scarcity of rented accommodation will naturally result in higher rents (unless there is interference with market forces by rent control), and in the view of economists, this is as it should be, for higher rents will eventually increase supply. They contend that where a tenant pays a lower rent, the subsidy is the amount of the difference between the market rent and rent actually paid, and it is a subsidy borne by the landlord.

There are, however, landlords who have not been concerned with profit, or with the views of academic economists. They are local authorities and housing associations, referred to variously as 'social housing' or 'the public rented sector'; and nowadays they provide over four times as many rented dwellings as do the private landlords. Their purpose has always been to meet the housing needs of people who cannot afford to buy or pay the sort of rents which a free market would require. Their primary concern has been to provide housing at rents which the average tenant can pay although such rents may not provide sufficient income to cover the cost of borrowing and of management maintenance. Hence the need for housing subsidies, whether in the form of annual payments towards the upkeep, or payments towards the initial cost of provision.

Central government and housing finance

Governments have always needed to know how much they had to raise to meet the calls that would be made on them and this used to be about all they did need to know. In modern times governments have also found themselves attempting, with varying success, to manage the economy. In this they have been concerned, among other things, with the share of the total national income (the Gross Domestic Product) which the public sector, national and local, will absorb. A large part of this sector's needs will be met by taxation and other revenues and the rest was referred to as the Public Sector Borrowing Requirement (PSBR). This PSBR was a constant cause for worry but it has now been replaced by GGE (General Government

Expenditure) which is defined as 'the amount which has to be raised by taxation or borrowing to finance the combined spending of central and local government including debt interest'. The Chancellor now worries about total needs, however they are met.

Each year a White Paper is published, called The Government's Expenditure Plans. This gives details of expenditure for each group of services (defence, social services, education, housing and so on) for the past five years and the current year, and what is planned for the next three years . The various tables cover local authority as well as central government activity.

The enormous mass of figures, analyses and supporting statements is intended to provide the basis on which the government's fiscal policy (how, and how much, is to be raised in taxes) and its borrowing requirement can be determined and it will also give the information needed for economic management.

Our concern is with housing. The figures for this are given in Table 12 (Table 9.1 of the White Paper, Cm 621, January 1989) and are set out, slightly abbreviated for reasons of space, on page 92.

In recent years there have been numerous changes in presentation, many of them improvements, one very important one being the removal of rent rebates and rent allowances from the housing programme to social security where they belong. Capital and current expenditure are now grouped separately whereas a few years ago they were mingled indiscriminately and confusingly. But another change is the glaring omission from the Housing Programme of mention of the tax relief for owner-occupiers, though it is now generally acknowledged that mortgage interest tax relief is a subsidy to house purchase. The cost of this was not actually included in the programme totals but it was at least given reasonable prominence in a note that followed. This has been discontinued. But, with perserverence, the student will find it tucked away unobtrusively in a final lengthy table of tax allowances and reliefs which comes after all the programmes. It will then be seen that tax relief on mortgage interest in 1990/91 cost £8,000 million, nearly three times as much as the entire housing programme for that year.

Then there is another important tax concession — the exemption from capital gains tax on house sales — also featured in that final table. The gross cost of this, estimated at £6,000m in 1987-88, leaps to a staggering £10,000m for 1988-89 as house prices spiral upwards. The net cost will be less, since presumably there would be allowances where the proceeds of sales are applied to the purchase of another house; but it must still be very significant.

Table 12

Department of the Environment
Housing Cash Plans
(£ millions)

	1986-87 outturn	1987-88 outturn	1988-89 estimated outturn	1989-90 plans	1990-91 plans
Gross capital expenditure					
Central Government					
Housing Corporation provision for rent by Housing Associations	684	696	731	813	1,080
Housing Association low cost ownerships	151	178	139	152	120
Other	3	3	4	4	—
Local authorities					
Public sector:					
Renovation	1,512	1,651	1,970	1,915	1,740
Provision for rent	612	626	650	540	390
Support for private sector					
Renovation & clearance	543	519	540	604	570
Lending to Hsing. Assns.	19	21	-5	10	10
Home ownership	78	82	90	85	80
New Towns	39	51	45	35	30
Total gross capital expenditure	3,641	3,826	4,163	4,158	4,030
Capital receipts					
Housing Corporation	-133	-125	-98	-114	-120
Other central government	-2	-4	-2	-2	—
Local authorities	-1,899	-2,190	-3,150	-3,490	-3,100
New Towns	-98	-143	-190	-195	-180
Total capital receipts	-2,132	-2,462	-3,440	-3,801	-3,400
Total net capital expenditure	1,509	1,364	723	356	630

	1986-87 outturn	1987-88 outturn	1988-89 estimated outturn	1989-90 plans	1990-91 plans
Current expenditure					
Central government					
Subsidies to:					
Housing Associations	29	36	43	51	60
Local authorities	534	473	520	487	480
Other Housing Corp., etc.	38	44	49	54	60
Local authorities					
Rate subsidies to:					
Local authority housing	422	477	441	428	440
Other	187	226	207	213	220
New Towns	85	83	80	53	50
Housing Action Trusts	—	—	1	68	90
Total current expenditure	1,296	1,339	1,341	1,354	1,400
Total Department of the Environment—Housing	2,805	2,703	2,064	1,710	2,030
Analysis by spending Authority					
Central government	1,304	1,301	1,386	1,445	1,680
Local authorities	1,473	1,412	743	304	360
New Towns	28	-10	-65	-39	-10
Total expenditure	2,805	2,703	2,064	1,710	2,030

Source: The Government's Expenditure Plans 1989-90 to 1991-92, January 1989, Cmnd 609

Comment: Note that in the first section, Gross capital expenditure, all the items in the Local authority group are financed by local borrowing or capital receipts. No government money is involved.

In the third section, Current expenditure, the second line lists the only payments made by central government in support of local authority housing. The later items under 'Local authorities' heading are council expenditure, not government subsidies.

For reasons of space two earlier years, 1984-5 and 1985-6 have been omitted, as has the latest 'plans' year, 1991-2. There has also been very minor merging of some small items.

Most important of all, and the least satisfactory, is the impression given that the programme totals represent resources provided by the government. They do not. In 1989-90, three-quarters of the gross capital expenditure in the housing programme was spent by the local authorities and it was their money that they were spending. No-one would dispute the government's need to know what share of the nation's resources will be required for central and for local government services. However, this is no justification for acting as though council spending, council revenues and council borrowing were all government transactions, carried out by local bodies on some sort of agency basis, and that council operations create the need for government borrowing or increased taxation just as much as if they were government operations.

Reform — A Range of Views

It should be obvious from what has gone before that the reform of housing finance is urgently needed. There are gross inequities between the different tenures and within them. Though they impose a considerable burden on public funds, the financial arrangements are singularly ineffective, and therefore wasteful, because of their failure to secure an adequate supply of accommodation, particularly rented accommodation.

In the private rented sector they do nothing to halt the decline in numbers, nor do they do enough to tackle disrepair.

As far as unfitness, disrepair and lack of amenities are concerned, the local authority sector actually has a rather better record than that of owner-occupied housing, and infinitely better than the private rented sector. Yet even here, the Association of Metropolitan Authorities has reported the need for spending some £19 billion in England alone; soon afterwards, the Audit Commission gave its estimate as £20 billion backlog in repairs and said that councils needed to double their spending to catch up.

As for home-ownership, the subsidy given by the taxpayer through tax relief continues its upward spiral. It is given automatically, whether there is need or not, gives most help to the better off, and in 1990/91 reached the astronomical figure of £8,000 million.

The present arrangements should also be a cause for concern, regarding the volume of savings which they absorb. In 1978, there were some 11.3 million owner-occupiers, and in that year, building society advances were £8,708 million. In 1988 there were 14.7 million owner-occupiers, a 23.4 per cent increase; but building society advances increased by 387 per cent to £43,441 million. Higher prices account for much of this enormous expansion but most of the money goes on financing the exchange of existing houses, not on building new ones. In 1978, one loan in five was on a new house; in 1989 it was one in ten. Clearly, changes of ownership have to be financed, and as prices rise, this costs more. But it is a sobering thought to consider what a small proportion of the vast volume of savings is actually adding to the housing stock.

Reform again on the agenda

After the demise of the Labour government in 1979, there was something of a lull in the reform debate, as the new Conservative government, while making it clear that there would be no change to tax benefits for owner-occupiers, brought in the 1980 Act changes to rents and subsidies in the council sector. Drastic cuts in investment followed, and the government showed no particular interest in the mammoth problems of homelessness, housing shortage, unfitness and disrepair.

In 1985, demands for action began to come in from all sides. In February, Roman Catholic bishops launched a national campaign drawing attention to these neglected issues, commenting that *'It is a shock to compare what has been given to those who have homes, and what has been withheld from those who do not'*.

In March a leading figure in the building society movement, Tim Melville-Ross of the Nationwide Anglia Building Society, referred to *'our crazy system of housing finance subsidy which favours owner-occupation to the detriment of every other form of tenure'*, and said that the way to a thorough and radical re-think of our housing policy is paved with the abolition of mortgage tax relief.

In April, the Royal Institute of British Architects followed up previous calls for action with *Decaying Britain*, an irrefutable case for vastly greater resources and a forceful condemnation of past neglect.

The Royal Institution of Chartered Surveyors came next with a discussion document, *Better Housing for Britain*, calling for heavy investment to increase the housing stock and tackle disrepair. They estimated an overall shortage of over a million dwellings. Financial arrangements should be changed. Tax relief on mortgage interest should be phased out. There should be a move towards market rents for both private and public rented sectors. Deficits or surpluses on council housing accounts should fall on, or accrue to, the Exchequer. Some controversial stuff here, but good to see the issues so forcefully argued.

The Duke of Edinburgh's report

In July 1985, there was a major contribution from a committee set up by the National Federation of Housing Associations (NFHA), chaired by the Duke of Edinburgh. *The Inquiry into British Housing* attracted wide attention, much of it directed to one recommendation, that mortgage interest tax relief was not justified and should be phased out. This was a pity, for it was only one of several equally important proposals.

The value of the report was in its comprehensive survey of the situation, the arrangements which had produced it, and the challenging solutions it proposed. It recommended a needs-related housing allowance to replace the tangle of housing subsidies, housing benefits for tenants, mortgage interest tax relief, and the housing element (as it was then) in supplementary benefit. This would put all tenures on the same footing.

For rents in all sectors, 'capital-value' rents were proposed, which would relate rents to current capital values, assuming vacant possession. This would give comparability between all rented dwellings, and while it would be set to give a reasonable return, it would not be as high as an unregulated market rent. It was claimed that nevertheless, rent income could be sufficient to attract private investment, thus reducing the dependence on government funds. Four per cent on current capital value was suggested as an adequate figure (interest rates at that time were about two per cent below today's), since the return, modest at first, would rise in line with house prices. It was accepted that capital-value based rents would not be practical without adequate housing allowances.

A change in the housing function of local authorities was also advocated. They would have a greater strategic and co-ordinating role but were not seen as the main providers of future rented accommodation.

By any standard, the NFHA report made a major contribution to the debate. Some of the principal recommendations, several of them controversial, will be referred to later.

'Faith in the City'

Finally in December 1985, there came the report of the Archbishop of Canterbury's Commission on Urban Priority Areas, *Faith in the City*.

As its title indicates, its primary concern was the problems of the inner cities, and there are sections on urban policy, poverty and unemployment, housing, health, social care, education, and law and order. The analysis, the message, the recommendations are relevant to our whole society. It is not possible to exaggerate its importance.

Its approach differed materially from that taken by the NFHA inquiry. The latter, while stressing the overwhelming need for a great expansion of building to rent, made proposals for reform which were largely shaped by the need, as the members saw it, to operate in the context of present government attitudes. Reform, therefore, assumed a continuing restraint on borrowing by local authorities, and the need for rents which would attract private investment. Income support subsidies rather than the general housing subsidies of the past were preferred; and an expansion of council provision was not favoured.

Faith in the City took an entirely different approach. It addressed itself to the social considerations on which housing policies should be based, to the principles which should inform the attitudes and actions of government and ourselves. Unlike the NFHA report, it lacked in concrete proposals for the finance of housing; but its importance lay in its examination of the fundamental deficiencies of existing policies and thinking which had brought us to the present situation.

Our society, the report said, has accepted that every citizen has a right to food, clothing, education and health care adequate to his or her needs, and irrespective of the ability to pay. Yet appropriate housing, which is as fundamental to human development as health care and having enough to eat, has never been accepted as a right for all. Although public housing was originally intended, with much success, to break the connection between bad housing and the ability to pay, it has never been funded adequately. Supply has never met demand, and too often council housing has been regarded as 'housing suitable for poor people'. And now that link between poverty and bad housing is being re-established.

Some argued that in any case, the public rented sector had failed. Paternalism in management had flourished. The Labour Party's traditional stance had been that council housing should be open to all who want it, but the resources had never been available to meet the demand, so there had been allocation on the basis of need and priority to low income families with children, resulting in unbalanced communities. Maintenance had been poor from the beginning, tenants had never been involved at any stage, capital costs had been reduced by putting dwellings on cheap inaccessible land and installing central heating systems as cheaply as possible. So the tenants were faced with very expensive transport and fuel costs, and the estates were called 'hard to let' — not 'hard to live in' — as if this was the tenants fault.

As for the private rented sector, it flourished when costs and interest rates were low, but investment in further provision ceased long ago. *Faith in the City* saw no future for an expansion of this tenure.

The voluntary housing movement had made only a small contribution to the national housing stock, the Commission found, but had an excellent record in its initiatives and in catering for special needs. It could be a significant force for the future but its financial dependence made it increasingly subject to government policy.

Government strategy relied heavily on home-ownership. The promotion of this was a deliberate political decision, encouraged by direct subsidy and by withdrawing of subsidy from council housing and pushing up rents. It was claimed that this had opened up choice. But *Faith in the City*'s view was that what characterised the housing conditions of low income people was lack of choice; and while owner-occupation did give maximum choice for those who could afford it, and made good financial sense for them, it will never be available to everyone. The cost of choice for the majority was the absence of choice for the minority who would never be able to buy.

The Commission was impressed by some small scale privatisation schemes of conversion from rent to owner-occupation. But they noted that the improvement needed to attract purchasers were the same as those the tenants wanted — security; 24 hour caretaking; the conversion of cramped three-bedroom flats into spacious homes for single people and childless couples. The Urban Development Grant, available towards the cost of the work if the private sector does it, was not available to the local authority.

In pointing the way forward, the Commission concluded that the housing problem cannot be contained, let alone reversed, without an expanded rented housing programme. Yet existing policies made housing bear the brunt of public expenditure cuts at a time when the decline in private renting was putting ever greater pressure on public renting.

Better standards were needed. A home is more than bricks and mortar, a roof over one's head. Decent housing means a place that is dry, warm, and in reasonable repair. It also means security, privacy, sufficient space, a place where people can grow, make choices, become whole people. The standards for public housing were ungenerous in space and appeared to assume that all the household except the woman and young children were out all day.

Co-operatives should be encouraged; management should be more responsive; maintenance and repair should have higher priority and funding.

Homelessness was a fearsome and rapidly growing problem, and the Homeless Persons Act should be amended so that it covered all the homeless, the report argued. The present categories were totally inadequate as a measure of need and should be abandoned.

These things all cost money, but the Commission said that if housing was regarded as a priority, money would become available. We were reminded that tax relief for house purchase, being regarded as income foregone rather than expenditure, was not subject to expenditure constraints. Yet it far exceeds the whole of the housing programme, capital and revenue together, in the government's annual public expenditure White Paper; and the cost to the community in lost tax revenue in assisting the purchase of a house was more than the cost to the community of providing a home to rent.

Faith in the City reminds us not merely of the size of the physical challenge, and the inequity and inefficiency of present arrangements, but also of the critical importance of decent housing to a just society; in short, of the thinking which should shape the reforms which are so urgently needed.

What the economists say

It is encouraging to be able to draw attention to a paper by two eminent economists, Professor M.A. King and A.B. Atkinson, published in the Midland Bank Review of May 1980. They took a very different view from that of most of their fellow economists, and had no difficulty in demonstrating the fundamental soundness of this country's past investment in public rented housing. They saw no reason for an increase in rent levels for this sector, though they thought national rent pooling needed consideration to reduce variations in rent levels between different housing authorities. They rejected the means-testing basis of the present housing benefit system; and suggested changes to the taxation arrangements which in their view favour owner-occupation to such a disproportionate extent. Reform, they said, is long overdue. All that is lacking is political will.

Ten years on, there is a further important contribution to the debate from John Muellbauer, the official fellow in applied economics at Nuffield College, Oxford, in the May + June 1990 issue of ROOF, Shelter's housing magazine.

He regards the current housing crisis as the most serious in a generation. Recent policy has been disastrous for the homeless and low income families. Letting prices rip in 1986-88, he believes, will come to be seen as one of the biggest blunders in post-war economic management. Prices and wages are rising; the balance of trade deficit is greater than ever before in peacetime; business investment is falling; and unemployment will soon be rising again. Yet there has been no sudden surge of inflationary pressures as has happened previously with oil and raw materials prices, and we need to look elsewhere for the causes of our troubles.

He considers that a key element lies in the obsession with providing incentives for owner-occupation. Land and house prices are inherently unstable and have been a source of difficulty for the economy before, and in the 1960s and 1970s these forces were kept in check by the rationing of mortgage and other credit. But this time, the policy was the opposite — financial liberalisation. He lists the main elements — abolishing exchange controls; lifting restrictions on the banks, which allowed their entry into the mortgage lending market, and the 1986 Building Societies Act which freed the societies from restrictions both on borrowing and on extending consumer credit.

The main effect has been to increase the spendability of illiquid assets, especially housing. This is now about 40 per cent higher than pre-1982, and the implied spending is way beyond the capacity of the economy to meet. Inflation and high interest rates have inevitably followed.

It was, he believes, astonishingly foolhardy to do all this while maintaining the key housing market distortion (deliberate incentives to owner-occupation at the same time as drastic reductions in building for the public sector and rents which are increasing relative to income).

The governments's response to every problem is to throw money at it, he says — housing benefit for low income families; the large subsidies of the Business Expansion Scheme to private landlords; tax relief and absence of capital gains tax for owner-occupiers.

The housing boom has collapsed but in a year or two there will be a recovery and then a repetition of the present state of affairs with even more damage to the economy.

If this is to be avoided, Mr. Muellbauer is convinced that lending criteria will need to be much more stringent, especially for second-time buyers. The unpopular poll tax should be replaced by a local property tax, on current market values instead of rents, indexed annually, and with a better rebates system. Mortgage tax relief should be reformed, and limited to the first eight or ten years of a mortgage as it is in Germany. It could be financed by a tax on more mature owner-occupiers.

This brief summary cannot possibly do justice to the forceful and challenging arguments put forward. They are certain to arouse controversy and lively discussion.

CERTAINLY I REMEMBER 'SOCIAL HOUSING'. WASN'T IT SOMETHING THE SALLY ARMY PROVIDED...?

THE ENVIRONMENT

PRESS

BRICK

council tenant opinion shows the opposite to be the case. None prefer a private landlord. A handful have opted for a housing association, perhaps encouraged by the prospect of large rent increases if they stay with the council, smaller ones if they transfer to an association. But most, wherever they are, prefer to stay with the council.

Moreover, if there is one thing that is self-evident, it is that councils are in a uniquely favourable position to provide houses in the numbers and quality required far more effectively than any other institution. They have the legal, financial, planning, architectural and engineering facilities and unrivalled experience. They built six million dwellings. With rising standards, many of these houses need improvement and would be getting it if government restrictions did not prevent this in most cases.

It is difficult to imagine any effective progress in the further provision of rented housing on the scale required, without the fullest involvement of a local government relieved of the dead hand of central government bureaucracy from which it now suffers.

Rents

To the present government the answer for the private rented sector is clear; market rents as soon as this can come about. The resulting chaos is going to be an embarrassment for any future government, but it will be thankful that the problem is a diminishing one as the sector continues to decline. At present the scarcity element provides a bonanza for anyone who cares to exploit it and rent control, in some form, should be reintroduced.

For councils and housing associations, the only sensible course is to reverse present policy, given that over half the tenants already need help from housing benefits and that the government's proposals for rents will make the situation worse. What justification can there be for rents reflecting ever increasing current values when tenants cannot meet the much lower rents based on the cost of provision? And it might be as well to remember that the greatest financial advantage of home-ownership is the avoidance of costs based on ever-rising current values. Why should tenants, as a class on much lower average incomes than mortgagors, be given fundamentally less favourable treatment?

The fact is that the system which local authorities developed for themselves, rents based on pooled historic costs and pooled housing subsidies, has been of inestimable benefit, socially and economically. The move towards rents which will mirror the huge variations in house prices in different areas is sheer folly.

Equally irrational and damaging is the new HRA subsidy, the new style HRA, and the virtually centralised control of housing authority policies. Separate housing subsidy and rent rebate subsidy replaced by a single HRA subsidy is intended to produce a situation in which continuing rent increases will remove any remaining housing subsidy element. As this is achieved, and rent increases continue, the rent rebate subsidy element will decline steadily. The cost of rent rebates (like rent allowances for housing associations and private landlords) has been rightly accepted as a social security function, to be borne by the whole community through the taxation system. Now the burden will be steadily transferred to the council as landlord — but not to private and association landlords — and through the council landlord to the tenants. The Treasury will be mightily pleased. This malign selective system needs to be scrapped with a restoration of subsidy which meets the full cost of rebates.

As time goes on, and assuming that incomes continue to rise, many local authorities will be producing surpluses because of the great advantage in owning large numbers of houses built long ago at much lower cost than today's. To what should these surpluses be applied? The government's answer is, to the general fund, as directed by the DoE. This is further discriminatory treatment of the public sector. The 'ring-fencing' absurdity should be removed at once, and freedom restored for councils to use surpluses to raise standards, improve services, or transfer to the general fund — whatever the local situation requires.

It is not simply a question of returning to the pre-1989 system, sensible though that was. On the one hand, the government is crassly set on a policy of widening the range of rents in different areas, while criticising the relatively modest differences between neighbouring authorities. It is time to look again at national rent pooling, or perhaps a subsidy system to give much needed help where land and building costs result in rents which are too far out of line with the general level.

As far as the housing association sector (a tenth of the size of the council sector) is concerned, the government clearly does not know what to do, with its vague talk of 'affordable' rents. There is no logic in two different rent systems, one for councils, another for the associations, both housing the same kind of families in generally the same kind of accommodation. The answer for housing associations, surely, is rent levels which are broadly similar to those of their larger neighbours, the local authorities.

Housing benefits

There is no likelihood that in the foreseeable future rent rebates or allowances, or some other form of income support, can be dispensed with.

What has been wrong with the present system is its detestable means test — so different from the automatic subsidy given by tax relief to mortgagors — and the repeated harsh amendments to the rules, euphemistically described as "more effective targeting". Other countries have had no difficulty in devising more humane systems, and in avoiding the deplorable 'poverty trap' element in our schemes. Reform is long overdue. The immediate reversal of the series of cuts in housing benefit since 1983, which imposed hardship on large numbers of low income families and gravely worsened the poverty trap, is of the utmost urgency.

At the same time, and no less urgent, there is the need to deal with the shocking plight of the thousands of single people, young and old, living in cardboard cities. They are deliberately excluded from the official designation of 'homeless', not even eligible for the miserable bed and breakfast accommodation which accommodates others who are marginally less unfortunate.

Subsidies for owner occupiers

The government and the opposition alike declare their dedication to the principle of tax relief on mortgage interest. The government will keep it as it is, tax relief at marginal rate, i.e. more help for the better off. The opposition is thinking about restricting it to standard rate.

There has not been any fiscal justification for this tax relief since 1963. Even the odd building society chief has said so recently. It cost £7 billion in lost tax revenue last year and will cost more still this year. If ever there was a waste of public money, this, under present arrangements, is it. There are various ways in which the burden can be reduced and help given more effectively.

There could, for instance, be tax relief limited to the cash value of the original mortgage. Is there any sense in giving relief, even if it is limited by a £30,000 mortgage ceiling, as at present, on every dwelling from a one bedroom flat to an enormous mansion? There could surely be a ceiling for eligibility. Then there was the Housing Centre Trust suggestion for what it called the 'single annuity' tax relief system. The first time buyer would get tax relief for the mortgage life, say 25 years; but if after, say, 7 years there was a move to another town, relief would be given on the new mortgage at year 8, not at year 1, and so on, ending altogether after 25 years.

There are many possibilities. Everyone accepts that it is in the early years of home-ownership that help is most needed. Some advocate relief on present lines but only for the first 10 years or so. An interest rate subsidy has been mooted to cushion drastic interest rate increases or take advantage of reductions. The present relief is a form of interest rate subsidy, but it gives a uniform rate of help, dependent as it is on the prevailing rate of income tax. An interest rate subsidy separated from the income tax system would enable housing assistance

114

and income tax policies to be operated separately, thereby allowing hard pressed mortgagors to be cushioned from high interest rates during periods of falling income tax rates.

There is the other separate but immense and growing tax privilege — the exemption from tax on the wealth represented by the owner-occupied dwelling. It is exempt from capital gains tax so long as it is the owner's principal dwelling, and there would be problems and strong opposition to taxing the increase in value so long as it is lived in by the taxpayer. However, there could, not unreasonably, be a housing wealth tax when a house changes ownership by inheritance, say at 25 to 40 per cent according to the marginal tax rate of the beneficiary. The inheritance of a dwelling is, it can be argued, a very real increase in personal wealth, and should be taxable.

No-one would think of ending present arrangements at one fell swoop. Clearly there can be savings; and clearly there can be more effective use of the money, the most glaring example being help to first time mortgagors at a more favourable rate than the rest. But whatever the changes, they will need to be phased in, and the best time to make them is when interest rates are being reduced.

But will it happen?

Without a change in present thinking, it will not. (The Welsh Secretary, David Hunt, has actually announced that he wants a further vast expansion of owner-occupation, and does not see why it cannot reach 90 per cent in the 1990s. He does not mention renting; or the homeless).

However, there is a new awareness, a rapidly emerging consensus amongst economists that the present housing policies are a disaster, not only for what they do or fail to do, but for the considerable part they are playing in the country's economic difficulties.

These difficulties show no sign of disappearing, and are indeed increasing. What is new, or at least what has been lost sight of for the last 10 years but is now re-emerging, is the close linking of housing policy with other vital policy issues which determine the overall economic and social management of the country, its future as one of the advanced industrial communities within Europe. It is no longer safe to ignore housing. The debate has begun. Change is on the way.

ndex